GUIDEBOOK
TO RELATIVE
STRANGERS

ALSO BY CAMILLE DUNGY

Trophic Cascade

Smith Blue

Suck on the Marrow

What to Eat, What to Drink, What to Leave for Poison

Black Nature: Four Centuries of African American Nature Poetry, editor

From the Fishouse: An Anthology of Poems that Sing, Rhyme, Resound, Syncopate, Alliterate, and Just Plain Sound Great, coeditor with Matt O'Donnell and Jeffrey Thomson

Gathering Ground: A Reader Celebrating Cave Canem's First Decade, assistant editor

GUIDEBOOK
TO RELATIVE
STRANGERS

JOURNEYS INTO RACE, MOTHERHOOD, AND HISTORY

CAMILLE T. DUNGY

W. W. NORTON & COMPANY
Independent Publishers Since 1923
New York | London

For information about permission to reproduce selections from this book, write to Permissions, W. W. Norton & Company, Inc., 500 Fifth Avenue, New York, NY 10110

For information about special discounts for bulk purchases, please contact W. W. Norton Special Sales at specialsales@wwnorton.com or 800-233-4830

Manufacturing by LSC Communications Harrisonburg
Book design by Chris Welch
Production manager: Julia Druskin

ISBN: 978-0-393-25375-7

W. W. Norton & Company, Inc.
500 Fifth Avenue, New York, N.Y. 10110
www.wwnorton.com

W. W. Norton & Company Ltd.
15 Carlisle Street, London W1D 3BS

1 2 3 4 5 6 7 8 9 0

For Callie. Now, always.
And for our fellow travelers.

CONTENTS

BY WAY OF INTRODUCTION

WHEN THE NATION that became the United States was beginning, women writers and black writers needed the endorse-
ment of other people in order to prove their legitimacy. Anne
Bradstreet, the first woman writer to publish a book out of the
American colonies, opened said book with testimonials from the
property-owning white men in whom her readers were bound
to believe. One of the stipulations surrounding the only book
ever published by the American colonies' first black woman
poet, Phillis Wheatley, was that the frontispiece must feature
the clarifying label "Negro Servant to Mr. John Wheatley of
Boston." And so it did. Expected of Frederick Douglass, Harriet
Jacobs, William Wells Brown—all key writers of the abolitionist
period—were what we have come to call "authenticating docu-
ments" attached to their books. The essays in the book you are
reading are steeped in such history.

I resist the implication that my own merits are not enough
to prove the worth of my words. Yet, I want to thank Jon Peede,

Kathryn Miles, Lucy Anderton, Sean Hill, Anna Lena Phillips Bell, Emily Smith, Jean Hegland, Lauren Crux, Tayari Jones, Dr. Lawrence Kaplan, and Dr. Nora McNamara. Your advocacy and attention helped move this book out of my study and onto the shelves. I owe a debt of gratitude to you, and also to Samantha Shea of Georges Borchardt, Inc., and Alane Mason of W. W. Norton.

This book was lifetimes in its production. A complete accounting of those who have aided and encouraged me seems an impossible—and improbable—task. Thank you to the late Mrs. Mudan, director of Foothill Montessori preschool, who taught me that I might be interested in many things at once and yet remain focused. Thank you to Mrs. Nichols, who, when I was in the seventh grade and smarter than a black girl was expected to be and, possibly for this reason, sometimes as disruptive as the literature allows, set me up as the teacher's assistant in our Honors English class rather than send me to the office. Thank you to Scott, the plainclothes security guard at University High who once lent me a copy of *The Autobiography of Malcolm X*. I can no longer recall what prompted his offering beyond the fact that we both enjoyed spending the lunch hour in proximity of the same shade tree. The book he gave me, I soon discovered, had been on my parents' shelves all along. Thank you to my parents and their bookshelves, my grandparents and their bookshelves, their parents and *their* bookshelves. It was no small thing to grow up knowing there was a body of literature that belonged to me.

Thank you to the sunset and the sunrise. I am not writing

this superfluously. There are too many of us who do not have the chance to see them.

Thank you to the people who made it clear that they hated me. Thank you to the people who made of themselves examples of the ways that, in the face of such anger, I could proceed.

This book is written toward a better understanding of moments when I have—and also have not—felt at home. Travel, like motherhood, calls my attention more acutely to new worlds I encounter and those I have left behind. Thank you to all who have welcomed me during my travels. I cannot name you all, for I am abundantly blessed.

Thank you Ben and Carolyn Van Zante, Bill Ford, Tammi Russell, Scott Cardwell, Rebecca Brown, and Laura-Gray Street. Thank you Priscilla Virant, Dr. Gerald McIntosh, and Sara Schaefer. Thank you Catherine Brady, Valerie Miner, Tess Taylor, Aimee Phan, Patricia Powell, Bich Nguyen, Xochiquetzal Candelaria, and Toni Mirosevich, who were there from the start.

Thank you to our neighbors, who sometimes plow the snow from our walk.

Thanks to everyone who aided me on the mountain.

Thank you to Nana Mary Quintela, Angharad Jones, Shannon Graham and Carlos DeLeon, Emily Bruce, Carrie Leilam Love, Matthew DeCoster, Charlene Hall, Rhowen Dalrymple, Barbara and Gene Ferguson, Papa Joe and Mama Maria, Misty and Mary, Allison and Alyssa, Ms. Shusta, Mrs. Tibbs, Mrs. Kalli Gladu, Dr. Giles, all the unnamed sitters and teachers, and Cole. The essays in this book—and, beyond the book, my whole life as a mother—would read quite differently without you. If you care for children, my child especially, you have my gratitude.

Thank you to Colorado State University, San Francisco State University, Randolph-Macon Woman's College (now Randolph College), the University of North Carolina at Greensboro, and Stanford University, the institutions where I have taught and learned. Thank you to all the colleges, universities, high schools, libraries, and other institutions that have invited me onto their campuses. Thank you to the Hermitage Artist Retreat, the Virginia Center for the Creative Arts, the Norton Island Eastern Frontier Society, the Sustainable Arts Foundation, the National Endowment for the Arts Fellowship Program, Ragdale, the Rocky Mountain National Park Artist-in-Residence Program, Blue Mountain Center, and the Djerassi Resident Artists Program. Thanks to Chris Merrill and the University of Iowa/U.S. State Department Outreach Tour, to Anthony Deaton and the U.S. State Department Speaker and Specialist Program, and to 49 Writers. Thank you Centrum, the Minnesota Northwoods Writers Conference, the Mendocino Coast Writers Conference, the Furious Flower Poetry Conference, Yari Yari Ntoaso, the Dodge Poetry Festival, Bread Loaf, the Bread Loaf Orion Environmental Writers Conference, the Napa Valley Writers Conference, Cave Canem, and Yaddo. If you are in any way responsible for making a haven for artists, thank you.

Thank you to all of the editors of the journals and anthologies who first accepted or encouraged these essays: *Virginia Quarterly Review, New England Review, Tupelo Quarterly, Shaping Memories: Reflections of African American Women Writers, Col-*

ors of *Nature, Rumpus Women, Ecotone, Black Nature, Wither,* and *Orion* magazine. Thank you to the archives and libraries and universities and books and articles and poems and podcasts and conversations that helped me write this book.

Thank you to Vanessa Holden and Mariama Lockington, to Beth Hessell and Lydia and Isaac, to Bayliss Camp and Drew Sutton, Janet Yu and Andrew McClelland, Kristen Schmid Schurter, Megan Lavelle, Megan McCarthy, and Megan Wilkerson, to Kim Wilson, to Rayshana Ali Black, to Regina and her family, to Dudley Edmonson, Drew Lanham, and Rue Mapp. Thank you to Aunt Ellie and Uncle Jim, to Mary Tesch Scobey, to Julie Black, to Uncle Jesse, to Uncle Edgar, to Aunt Jeannye, to my dear cousins, and to all my relatives, whom I love. There are people who believe the writer's talent is individual, but I understand myself to be indivisible from the people I relate to and from the people related to me. Thank you to my sister, Dr. Kathryn Dungy, and her husband, Tim Voigt; to my grandparents, all of them; to Mom and Dad, the Drs. Claibourne and Madgetta Dungy. Above all, I offer love and gratitude to my husand, Dr. Ray Black, and to my daughter, Callie. Kinship with you has made me.

THE CONSCIENTIOUS
OUTSIDER

A n artist goes to an artists' retreat, or colony as they are often called, to get away from the things that typically sideline her in life: insistent phone calls, cooking, dusting, running errands, preparing lectures for class. I was not yet married and was nobody's mother, but my work/life balance was frequently tipped in ways that hindered the artistic pursuits that both economically and emotionally sustained me. Within the retreat's carefully constructed atmosphere of tranquillity, I was free for a month to focus on writing.

When two of my fellow colony guests began to talk over dinner about *The Hours,* I stayed mum. For one thing, they were talking to each other, not to me. Furthermore, I was on a retreat, and I didn't feel like putting energy into explaining why I hadn't seen the film or read the book. I'll tell you now, from everything I'd seen, heard, and read, the story struck me as slightly overwrought and, well, white, and I hadn't mustered the mood or time to care about it. But it's hard to explain to a table full of white folks that sometimes I'm just not interested in spending time or money on films and books that focus on the melancholy of the white experience.

The lesbian writer hadn't seen the film, either.

Let's not call her "the lesbian writer." The other is too frequently identified by that which sets her apart. I don't want to follow that convention. Let's give her a name. Let's call her Seattle.

Seattle's motives for not having seen the film were more carefully reasoned than mine, a fact I learned because she was pressed to justify her position to her fellow colony guests in a conversation she later referred to as "the one where I was backed into a corner like a hissing, feral beast." This despite the fact that her initial proclamation of disinterest in the film had been made in the context of a dialogue with just one other person. We'll call him DuPont Circle.

Opening her conversation to the table, Seattle laid out the basic reasons she had not seen the film, several of which had to do with its representations of lesbians. In a point related to her argument, Seattle asked us to name ten out lesbian actors working prominently in Hollywood. This was 2003. I want to believe that in the intervening years things have changed for the better, so I challenge you to play along at home. The party at our dinner came up with Ellen DeGeneres and Rosie O'Donnell. Seattle said, "I'd like to point out that neither one of those women was comfortable coming out publicly until she had solidified her career. Still, that's two. I asked for ten names." No one had anyone else to add. "I'll make it easy on you, just give me three more." People mentioned Jody Foster, but at the time she wasn't out.

"But L.A. is totally progressive! Are you trying to suggest that Hollywood is closed to gays and lesbians?" asked a writer from Long Island.

"I'm just looking at the numbers," said Seattle. "Tell you what. You're a writer. Name some lesbian writers whose work gets talked about these days."

There were six actively publishing writers at the table. The poet from the north of England knew no one, DuPont Circle named two authors, and I nodded to second Pacific Palisades' nominee. That brought us to a total of three names.

"I haven't heard of any of those people," said our girl from Long Island.

"My point exactly!" Seattle pounded her fist on the table, thinking our lack of familiarity had confirmed something.

I felt vindicated in my disinterest in a film about middle- (to upper-middle-) class white women. My indifference to other people's anxieties was not, apparently, unique. The general lack of knowledge the table betrayed about lesbian literature and film confirmed my suspicion that Americans often don't care much about the things that concern people who aren't like them. The difference, as Seattle's situation made clear, is that, whereas the conscientious outsider will likely expend some thought and care justifying her reasons for not seeing a film that (mainstream) critics and audiences agree is the film of the season, the mainstream masses don't bother with realities that don't concern them.

Even that word—*mainstream*—troubles me. Who decides

which stream should be the central stream, the authoritative path, for depictions of our diverse worlds?

Consider a friend of mine who, three weeks into the fall semester of his second year as a student in a prestigious creative writing graduate program, found himself so dejected he felt compelled to call me at the artists' retreat. "Half my poetry craft class has dropped. Half! Today, I overheard one guy repeat three times that he *would have* dropped except the class was 'stupid and easy' and so he was going to stick around."

The course was being taught by a young-appearing African American woman who boasted, among her many qualifications, several books, a Guggenheim, a faculty post at an Ivy League institution, numerous teaching awards, and a position on the Board of Governors of the Poetry Society of America. Her syllabus consisted primarily of books by black women writers. My friend was relatively certain that the people who had dropped the class, all white, and predominantly male, had done so because they just couldn't stand to be, as he termed it, "decentered." A sister was teaching a class about writing by black women. Clearly, the content would be "stupid and easy," if not downright unworthy of the time. What could black women possibly teach about the craft of poetry?

Back in the colony's dining room, our friend from Long Island added perspective. "Maybe no one's talking about these writers because they're not any good." She was certain this explained her (give it a name) ignorance. If a thing hadn't crossed her threshold of experience it must not be worth noticing. She took a large bite of pie and smiled through pink lipstick.

I uttered my first words of the evening, which were something like, "Christ Almighty!" and left the table under the guise of returning my plates to the kitchen.

When I came back, the seventh member of our company, a composer from Williamsburg, was beginning to understand Seattle's point. "This is sort of like blacks in Hollywood. For so long there were so few and the only roles they could play were maids."

"No black woman has played a maid in a movie for, like, twenty years," said Mrs. Long Island.

In my normal life as a professor I give lectures on the representation of black women in American film. I had numbers and films to dispute her claim. But I was at an artists' retreat, not in the classroom. I was supposed to be able to get away from my normal life. Why should I have to be the expert tonight?

"Maybe not maids exactly," said Williamsburg, "but the point is that there was a limited opportunity for many years and that limited opportunity meant that there was a limited scope of representation for blacks. Isn't that right?" He turned to me.

Williamsburg was on the path Seattle had tried to pave, but things could turn against her again at any moment. "Help me out here," Seattle pleaded.

There's no way around it. When you are the only one at the table, eventually they will always turn to you. "Right," I said.

It had been barely five days since I'd completed the twenty-eight hours of travel that returned me from my first extended trip to Ghana. I was still jet-lagged. I was feeling a little queasy even before the conversation began. I wanted to make as short work of my involvement as possible. "Sure," I continued.

"What are you talking about?" Long Island was incredulous. "There is a load of opportunity available to black people in Hollywood today! Didn't Halle Berry just win an Oscar?"

In the history of the prize, only Halle Berry, as a highly sexualized conduit for the redemption of a white man, has won an Oscar for best leading actress. At the time of our conversation at the artists' colony, the other two Oscars, for best actress in a supporting role, had been awarded to black women for roles in which they were conduits for the redemption of white people (Hattie McDaniel—as a maid—and Whoopi Goldberg—as a medium). This was before Jennifer Hudson, who had the opportunity to serve as a conduit for the love life and redemption of light and lovely Beyoncé Knowles; before Octavia Spencer, who, in 2011, played a maid; and before Lupita Nyong'o, who played a slave. Of the seven black women who have won an Academy Award for acting, the only exception to this pattern has been Mo'Nique. One entertainment news outlet reported that, as Mary Jane in *Precious*, Mo'Nique "wore no makeup and even grew hair under her arms" so she could play the role of an abusive mother who was ugly outside and in. That night at the artists' colony in New York, I told the table what I knew about the poor odds of a black actress winning the favor of the academy if she didn't play the help.

"But black people are the mainstay of popular American culture. The movies, hip-hop, everything. Everybody wants to be a part of black culture. Everybody loves it. Both my sons are dying to be black."

There was too much in Long Island's statement for me to tackle at once. Speechless, I sat with what I thought was a blank face.

"Why are you blinking your eyes at me that way?" She was a mother. She was used to identifying faces like mine: contempt in the guise of indifference.

"Give them two days as a black person," I suggested. "See what they think after that."

I was full of fear for these boys from Long Island. They had no idea what they were hoping to get into. And how could they? When and how and why did they embrace black as something they wanted to be? Did the black people they so admired come from staid middle- (to upper-middle-) class families like the one in which I was raised? Likely no. Likely, there was some other experience they were after. When did they first start noticing black people, and when they noticed us, what was it they thought they discovered?

At the end of my first three weeks in Ghana, I found myself in a house with a satellite television system tuned to CNN. I watched the U.S. news for over an hour, then I flipped to a local station and caught the end of a Ghanaian commercial wherein a big-boned black woman walked into a room and every man whistled in admiration. At this point I realized what had been odd about watching the U.S. network after several weeks of not watching American TV. Hitherto, the only television I had watched in Ghana had been either the news broadcast each evening by Ghana TV or *Big Brother Africa*. (There were eight contestants left when I started watching, only one of whom was white.) The images I saw in television programs, commercials, billboards, and magazines were almost exclusively black, and I could wander around the city for several days without seeing a white face. Outside of the historical context that can't be ignored in a former Portuguese, Dutch, and British colony, it got so I hardly thought about white people. I loved it when people spoke to me in Twi, assuming I would understand the local language. What a relief it was to see people like me at every turn, not to be the obvious outsider, for a change. But, when I'd watched CNN, I had only seen white people.

When you belong, you can overlook the totality of otherness, the way that being other pervades every aspect of a person's life. That night in the New York artists' retreat, I wasn't yet worried about how all this willful ignorance and erasure would affect my little black girl, as yet unconceived. I was only concerned with myself. I was thinking about how race directs the course of all my actions. My taste in films, who I befriend, the things I choose to write about, all are influenced by the particular position (or number of positions) I occupy in American culture. My otherness manifests itself in what I eat, what I watch, what I read, what lipstick I can wear, where I can walk unmolested.

Our conversation happened to take place in a privileged space—where the work requested of me was to think and to write—but I have had similar conversations at the office, the grocery store, at church, the nail salon, while washing dishes (my own and other peoples'), at the gas station, the dentist's, a Super Bowl party, in restaurants and bars, with my daughter's child-care providers, with supervisors who would oversee the advancement of my career, with roommates or lovers with whom I was expected to share my nights and days, during long walks on the beach, and in heated interactions over the copy machine.

This is a set of exchanges you can't get away from if you live in America in a body that looks like mine.

"Look," I said. I was in the conversation now. I might as well try to help Seattle prove her point. "I am the only black person at this table, which means that I have become the representative of blackness here."

"I don't see you as *a black woman*. You're just who you are." Long Island's nod of support suggested that Pacific Palisades had taken the words from between her pink-glossed lips.

I've made the readjustment almost completely now, I wrote a friend after I'd been back from Ghana awhile. *I am feeling very American again*. Being home means being able to predict the direction an argument will take.

I am certainly who I am (an ornery individual at the moment), though I take umbrage at the idea of limiting my scope with a word like *just* when it is used to suggest I am a simple person. If I may borrow a phrase from the great poet of our early democracy, "I am large, I contain multitudes." *Just* in this context erases various complexities and dimensions of my being. There is a danger in refusing to, or tacitly agreeing not to, recognize my black womanness. Black womanness is part of what makes me the unique individual I am. To claim you do not recognize that aspect of my personhood and insist, instead, that you see me as a "regular" person suggests that in order to see me as regular some parts of my individual identity must be nullified. Namely, the parts that aren't like you. This argument has been made before. I made it again.

"The fact of the matter is that I am the only person of color at this table. The fewer people there are to represent a particular segment of a population, the less likely it is that accurate, or diverse, perceptions will be drawn about that population." And the more likely, I thought but did not say, that one individual will be asked to speak for the lot. I was in this odd position of both defending and shaking my claim as spokeswoman for the race because someone singled me out. This happened, in turn, because another outsider felt compelled to justify her (hitherto private) decision not to see a film at which she took offense. Seattle was lesbian spokeswoman for the night, and as resident black girl, mouthpiece for the disenchanted masses, I was called upon to back her up.

When you are a conscientious outsider, dinner can be a dangerous and tiring affair.

When I first got back from Ghana, I was ready to turn around and go right back. I had felt a sense of comfort and freedom there that surpassed any happiness I'd known before. There is something undeniably relaxing about being phenotypically one of many (or most) rather than one of few (if any). Perhaps it would be a more stable world if everyone could experience both the sensation of oneness and that of otherness a few times in life. A person who isn't reminded several times a day about the implications of the color of her skin has time to consider the implications of other things. Having lived a life where my outsider status is called to my attention on a regular basis, it was a noted pleasure to blend into the crowd. In Ghana, I was left free to discover the possibilities of so much unmolested psychic space.

The artists' colony is constructed to serve a similar goal: to provide a space in which the creative mind can roam unfettered. But considering the conversations that implicated me at dinner, over ping-pong, while walking up the stairs to my bedroom, or while waiting for my breakfast egg, it was difficult to let my mind feel at ease.

There were two sources of experience for the poems I found myself writing at the colony. One set of poems was based on narratives of black people held in or self-emancipated from slavery. The other poems were about visiting the giant fortresses on the coast of Ghana, from whence slave ships left for the Americas. This work was a startling reminder of the many implications and tolls of otherness and erasure.

At breakfast one morning, several of the guests waxed delighted about how their rooms were cleaned regularly, "as if by fairies." We were living in a mansion. So as to allow us time to create, our meals were cooked for us, our bathrooms scrubbed. We were invited, for the duration of our stay, to behave as if the mansion and its amenities were our own.

There is something about privilege that can place one in a position to erase the realities of others. Those weren't fairies pushing the vacuum cleaner and cleaning my tub. They were women with lives and flesh and families and histories. My life and flesh and family and history demand that I recognize them where and how I can.

MANIFEST

———

can say: That is a hawk. But not: red-tailed, red-shouldered. I can say: deer. But not: white-tailed. I can say robin. I can say raven. I can say bird, but not: bunting, wren, warbler. Sometimes: gerbera daisy. Sometimes: crimson glory rose. But not the name of the creeper that edges my neighbor's lawn or the flowering stands near the car park.

I can say blackberry in every season: fruit, flower, and vine. I can say poison oak. I can say: Watch out for the thistle. But not what the berries are that grow at the base of the park's redwood trees. (I can say redwood. I can say *Sequoia sempervirens*.)

I can say: California poppy, nasturtium, tiger lily. Eastern fox squirrel (like me, not native). I know so much about this part of California, but if I had to make my way to you by naming everything that I encountered, I'd never make it home.

I want to say border collie, not just dog. I want to say king snake, not just snake. I want to say aloe and agave, not just cactus, which would, anyway, be imprecise. I notice, now more than ever, what I don't know, and what I want to know, and what I want to share with you, Callie Violet. I want to name the world correctly. One day this will be your language, and I will have been the first to present it to you.

•

THERE IS A STORY I HEARD, when you were the tiniest baby, about a waiting room in someplace close to Heaven. After death, that is where people go to wait to be forgotten. A place where people would want to stay for a while. No one wants to be immediately forgotten. Family might reunite in the room, if I remember the story correctly. I imagine enemies would confront each other there, too.

When we mourn, we give memory a name, and in this room those memories were corporeal. It feels like a long time ago, when you were the tiniest baby and I listened to the story while we drove from one place to another.

For a while, the bodies thought it was nice to be in the waiting room. It was nice to be remembered. But after a while, names lose meaning. Living speakers stop associating some real body with the body's name. In the waiting room in the place close to what we might call Heaven, a man who drowned in a New England well waits to be forgotten, while every day a tour guide on some idyllic college campus walks by the well and repeats, with less tenderness than she bestows upon the well stones, the still-not-completely-forgotten man's name.

Naming is a kind of claiming. In the Judeo-Christian tradition that is your inheritance, Adam named all the birds and beasts of the world, including Eve. Even after his exclusion from the Garden, even after the all-consuming loss he suffered when he acquired the deeper knowledge that brought on his expulsion from Eden—and hardship and death—Adam possessed the names of everything with which he'd once shared uncomplicated communion. The ability to name even a lost world keeps that world alive. I imagine this was both painful and potent for Adam, who, like the drowned man in the story I only half recall, must have wanted some days to return completely to the world he remembered. That world was gone, though. In reality, if not in memory, his past was irrevocably erased.

·

YOU ARE NAMED CALLIE VIOLET after my grandmother, Callie Madge, and your father's grandmother, Violet. You are my grandmother's first great-grandchild, and there was no question that you would be Callie. My grandmother's grandmother was also a Callie, and now our family spans three centuries through one name.

It was the continuity I wanted. Persistence personified.

Some people are surprised I named you after someone who was still alive. What if the angel of death came for the old one, got confused, and took you instead? I want to say this never occurred to me. But sometimes I worry that I left no room for you, my daughter, in this old woman's name.

When you came to be outside my body, the name we bound you to seemed limiting.

I call you Abena because you were born on a Tuesday. I call you Abeni because the name means we asked for her and she has arrived. These are Fante and Yoruba names, for these, too, might have been your people.

The next time I hold you, I call you Butter Bean because, when you were a newborn package of squirm and gas smiles—my stinky little Cochina—you, like three of your great-grandmothers before you, were the color of a butter bean.

There is no escaping history.

Your aunt calls you Minukee, a Louisiana Creole endearment with Afro-indigenous roots. She calls you mon petite chou, my little cabbage, my precious little girl.

Because you coo-coo-coo in the morning, you are my Mourning Dove. Not just any old bird.

Your godmother calls you the Boo Boo, because that is what her father called her and so that is how she knows to show you love. Your grandfather, using all your initials, calls you CVDB. I call you CV.

I call you Argentina, because I do not want you to cry. Your father calls you Little Bit.

The act of naming who you are to us may never end.

•

I WALK WITH YOU DAILY because the confines of our apartment are too small.

I point out the trees we walk beneath: plum, crab apple, lemon, mulberry. Eat this, not that, eat this not that, I tell you, as if it is never too early to teach you what might cause you the most harm.

I want you to know a violet when you see one, Callie Violet, and though they are lovely, just as you are lovely, I want you to know the calla lilies growing in every other Bay Area garden have nothing to do with your name.

Rhododendron, rose, I say, daisy, daisy, chrysanthemum.

White flower, purple flower, pretty yellow flowers, because I cannot name them all. The walk is long, the hill is steep, and I am often out of breath.

•

Ma Ma Ma Ma Ma Ma Mama is your latest sound, and I've known better than to think that when you made that sound you made it for me. But today you looked at me when you said, *Ma Ma Mama*, and when I came toward you and lifted you up off your play mat, you giggled and repeated the words that had brought me to you: *Ma Ma Mama*. And just that quickly, I had a name.

The jury is still out on whether your infant brain can consciously drive action in the way that my brain receives the things I see. A jellyfish swimming in my direction is not consciously moving toward me. A mosquito who favors my skin over your father's may be responding to higher levels of carbon dioxide, not making a statement about my relative sweetness. In both cases, the hard-line objectivist will assure me that what might feel like intentional attention is not. Electrical signals, hormonal imperatives, these drive action. Not emotion or reason or thought.

These same hard-line objectivists are liable to tell me that animals do not *feel* in the same way humans feel. Without the capacity for language, a dog or a whale or a stork is incapable of human emotion. To say a stork is sad when it loses its mate is to risk anthropomorphizing, to lose scientific objectivity, and to falsify the intellectual potential of the stork. But I will not make distinctions between emotional capacities based solely upon what we know of language. I know the orphaned elephant wakes with nightmares, *knowing* what happened to her herd, and *mourning* that loss. This is why the caregivers of orphaned elephants sleep with the foundlings, so they do not have to wake up afraid and alone. I know that whales express gratitude when released from a bind. I know that captive baboons store anger and express it, intentionally, with the calculated hurling of poop.

I know that you are only now acquiring English, after hearing us speak it during your six months out of the womb and forty weeks inside. I know that the *Ma* sounds, like the *Da* sounds from earlier this month, are merely your way to explore the range of sounds available to you. When the sounds first started, I had no illusions that you meant anything by the expressions. But I know, also, that you are smarter than I have the capacity to understand, and I know that when you look at me and make a sound, and when I recognize the sound and respond, and when you repeat my new name without losing eye contact, this is not an accident. And I am filled with unspeakable gladness.

O NE OF THE EASIEST WAYS to strip a person of her power is to take away her right to choose her name.

The Interesting Narrative of the Life of Olaudah Equiano, or Gustavas Vassa, chronicles an eighteenth century man's journey from an African (Igbo) boyhood through the seas and hands and lands of Europe and its colonies. In the book, the young protagonist is forced to answer to at least four different names. In his own abolitionist autobiography, Frederick Douglass writes about resisting renaming. So do Solomon Northup, Harriet Jacobs, and characters imagined—with the help of a narrative written by Josiah Henson—by Harriet Beecher Stowe. Abolitionist literature is riddled with stories of people who recognize that freedom is measured, in part, by the freedom to choose one's own name.

When we take a man's name, he disappears. Sleeping car porters in the twentieth century were referred to, by white passengers in the segregated train cars where these porters worked, as "George." This is if they were referred to by any name at all other than "boy" or "you there" or some more brutally dismissive term. A man in prison is sometimes known only by his number. In many morgues, a body without a history is called John or Jane Doe.

At some point you will decide what the world should call you. Callie or Callie Violet or some other, as yet undetermined, name. I can't know what the future will name you, but when I call you Sweet Pea or Turtle Dove, Abena or Pumpkin, Callie Violet or my sweet girl, I do it always in the same tone, so you have learned to turn when I speak. I think you turn not to the names but to the sound of my voice when I speak your many names, the sound I hope you already recognize means you are truly and completely loved.

.

I LOVE WHEN YOU NOTICE ME, when you direct a new skill toward me as if to purposefully engage me in your growth. When you learned to kiss me, I felt as if every expression of love I'd ever directed toward you had been returned sevenfold. Now you pull my face toward yours and, with your mouth wide as a whale shark's, smooch my chin or cheek or forehead, whatever part of my face happens to be near. This must be what my mouth feels like on your face, my lips covering huge portions of your skin. Yesterday, you pulled back and reapplied your smooch several times, as if to duplicate my *muah muah muahs*. Sevenfold times sevenfold times sevenfold, that blessing.

When you meet someone new, you meet them as a blind person might meet someone who matters. You lift your little hand to the new face and work it over the eyes and the nose, the mouth, the cheeks. You learn the contours of the primary points of interaction, and when you are satisfied with what your hands have learned, you smile, maybe even coo. This is how you say hello to strangers and to whatever it is we parents and guardians are to you. Lovers? We kiss you so much, cuddle you and caress you, we *love on you*. Sometimes your kisses catch me full on the lips, and I wonder when I will need to teach you not to show your affection in this way. I try to turn my face lest my hunger for your displays of affection appear indecent.

We are not supposed to conflate these two worlds of physical affection: the kisses and intimate touches of the lover of the body and the kisses and intimate touches of the lover of the babe. But it is like that. I take big whiffs off the top of your head, let your hair tickle my chin. I want you close close closer. When I am with you, mon petite chou, I feel good good and close and happy. I'm not talking about a kind of sexual good good feeling, though what I am talking about is mixed up in the same general neighborhood, which is why this feels like such a dangerous thing to be saying, to be feeling, to be acting upon. I'm talking about a *good* good feeling. A forever kind of good feeling. A whatever you need, whatever you want, take it, I don't ever intend to be too far from you again good feeling. I'm talking about feeling like you make me feel—you make my brain and my heart feel—better than I've ever felt.

I think I was expecting you to kiss like a guppy might kiss, swift cold pecks that were nearly imperceptible. But, little whale shark, you devour me.

When you take hold of me on the far side and pull my head toward yours, the force is sometimes so strong I can hardly believe you are only a six-month-old baby. Sometimes, when you hold me like that, or when you resist being held, my mind flashes to stories of smothered children, and I understand how intentional those crimes have to be, how actively a person would have to work to overpower even an infant's resistance. This is what happens when I am with you, Mourning Dove. I can be intensely in the presence of our pleasure when your mortality manifests, a specter undeniable as my joy when you slay me with kisses.

.

ON FEBRUARY 4, 1846, a ship called the *Brooklyn* left New York with 238 voyagers, mostly Mormons from the East Coast. After being blown nearly to Cape Verde, after being caught in the doldrums in the South Atlantic, after rounding Cape Horn without incident, then being gale-blown south again, after detouring nearly four hundred miles from their desired dock at Valparaiso and stopping over in the Juan Fernández Islands, after taking on fresh water, fruit, and salted fish, after burying one dead woman in the earth the islands offered, after more time on the Pacific, after laying over in the Sandwich Islands, after leaving one woman and her mortally ill infant son on Oahu, after many more days on the open ocean, after nearly twenty-four thousand miles, on July 3, 1846, the *Brooklyn* docked at the small settlement of Yerba Buena, its passenger load more than doubling Yerba Buena's population.

The Mormon settlers arrived just as United States forces seized control of California. Within a year the growing settlement, once called Yerba Buena, was officially known by

its current name. Now when we say Yerba Buena in relationship to the San Francisco Bay area, we don't mean the community that grew up near what we call Mission Dolores in the
city we now call San Francisco, but the small island through
which runs the tunnel portion of the San Francisco–Oakland
Bay Bridge.

In 1846, there were only village ruins on this island, aban-
doned pots and pestles. Tuchayunes had buried their dead in
the hillside sitting up, knees tucked near their chins. But these
are not things the people who came off the *Brooklyn* would have
known when they docked and took up camp near the settlement
at the mission.

The new arrivals might have known the island as Goat Island,
as some did at the time and for many years after, though there
was a fairly effective slaughter of the goats that had earned the
island that name. Spanish-speaking settlers called it Isla de
Yerba Buena. Some U.S. surveyor must have liked the sound, for
Yerba Buena Island remains the official name. No one for a long
time has called the outcropping Sea Bird Island, nor have they
used the word the Tuchayunes would have used to call it by that
name. The padres at Mission San Francisco de Asís had already
killed most of these First Californians with overwork, unfamiliar diet, and European disease.

It was to ward off ill health that the Tuchayunes used the California mint, the "good herb," whose vines trailed around the
mission settlement and also draped the island in the bay. People say tea steeped from yerba buena tastes like a cross between
mint and pine. Perhaps someday I'll make a cup for you.

BABIES ARE LIKE CHOCOLATE. Like that first bite of a phenomenal steak. That rich and savory. Delicious. Umami and sweet. Umami most of all, that fifth, most crucial, taste Westerners loved but didn't have a name for until the word *umami* migrated to us. To get to umami we have to stew meat all the way down to the bone. I am talking about love. Consuming love. I am not talking about oppression, suppression, or power plays, though I am aware of how all these things could manifest and corrupt the love that I love. I am talking about acknowledging our animal desires, both yours and mine. When you kiss me, Sweet Pea, I want to eat you up.

Reading a passage about running or eating cinnamon activates the same parts of our brain as would be activated if we were actually running or eating cinnamon. When I say I am going to eat your little baby thighs and little baby stomach, the parts of my brain that activate when I eat something delectable must go wild. You kiss me, and I am hungry for more kisses.

Since you came to live inside me, much of my sense of propriety is gone. It is as if there were many doors to our apartment. Every door is open, and anyone can walk inside. Strangers talk to me about their own incontinence and I tell them about my weeping breasts. Women I don't know walk into my bathroom to double-check my strategy for mitigating hemorrhoids. Nothing is private. Nothing is sacred. There is nothing I keep to myself. Being your mother has required one act of vulgarity after another, and I am so strung out on you I couldn't care less.

I don't know if I can define myself anymore, now that I'm your mother. You've consumed me. Being your mother has cooked me right down to the bone.

·

Your Grandmother Julie, far more restrained than your mother, has devised a greeting that doesn't involve kissing but allows for eye contact and smiles. When your Grandmother Julie was here, she taught you to press your forehead to hers. She never threatened to eat you up. We all have our own ways of telling you we love you.

You picked the gesture up in one day and every time Grandma Julie was near, you'd run your little hand over her nose and brow ridge, and then you'd bump your tiny forehead right against her head. She was proprietary about this demonstration of affection. She would tell you and anyone around that this was how *she* greeted you. None of the rest of us gets your forehead pressed against our foreheads. It's your secret handshake with your Grandmother Julie.

Your father and I get the wide-mouthed kisses. Soon you'll be waving like your Grandmother Dungy when your Grandmother Dungy is around. Already you are flapping your little hand, rotating at the wrist and collapsing the fingers toward the pad of your palm, in the specific way your Grandmother Dungy gestures, *Hello, my love*, and *Goodbye, my love*, and *I'll see you soon, my little darling*. What is language but the way we communicate with each other? You are already multilingual, aware of the proper greetings for the various micro-cultures you come in contact with. As we would be if we were in a foreign country and heard someone call us in our native tongue, when we are in your world, we are always delighted that you make the effort to greet us in a way we understand.

Around you, I *am* in a foreign land: the land of infancy, with its particular laws and language. With its specific names for things. Its confounding customs. Like an American who lives for a while someplace where the plumbing consists primarily of pit toilets and buckets for hand-washing, I've learned both that I need not be grossed out by human waste and that there are more or less sanitary means to discard of it. So much of my energy is taken up learning new information that I am tired tired tired all the time. I have nearly given up dreaming, and when I do dream, even my dreams seem foreign to me, and so I cannot rest when I am sleeping.

Tired as I am, I am that much more susceptible to emotions. I think that must be why, most of the time, I feel like I'm strung out. Living in your country has exhausted me beyond the point of reason.

•

I WORRY ABOUT THE END DAYS more now than I did before you were born. Your father has humored me and put track shoes, old jeans, and a T-shirt in a go-bag. In case of earthquake or firestorm, I keep food, water, and a basic first-aid kit in an accessible place.

I am teaching myself to identify edible native plants. The berries on bay laurel can make a substitute for coffee. Acorns can be soaked and leached and mashed into a nutritious paste. Miner's lettuce, which restaurants are serving in $20 salads, comes up along the creek path after rains. I've always liked to season my own salads with nasturtiums. Though it's native to Mexico and South America, nasturtium has made itself at home in Northern California. The yellow-orange flowers add a peppery taste to greens and brighten the plate.

Juan Bautista de Anza, Junípero Serra, Fermín Lasuén, and the other colonists who walked to Northern California, planting missions and settlements and cutting the road we still call El Camino Real, sowed mustard seeds along the way, enacting the parable from Matthew, Chapter 13. *"The kingdom of heaven is like a mustard seed, which a man took and planted in his field. Though it is the smallest of all seeds, when it grows, it is the largest of garden plants and becomes a tree, so that the birds come and perch in its branches."* California, in the blooming season, is vibrant with mustard's many-headed bracts of yellow flowers, on which I have often seen birds perch.

The Mediterranean grasses that cover the hills of California, historians think, came on the fetlocks of livestock.

Mormons were the first to grow wheat here.

Wild fennel, which must have been cultivated in some early settler's garden, grows all around.

Sausal Creek runs behind our apartment, flowing down from foothills where—for centuries—*Sequoia sempervirens* were rooted. Along the creek path, native and exotic blackberries grow wild. Fruit trees thrive in the places where loggers and the farmers who came after the loggers once chucked their pits.

Fennel, blackberry, mustard, plum: I point these out on our walks. We can eat these if we need to, I say. As if naming what could save us might save us one day.

•

Most states and territories in America were inhospitable to adherents of the word of God as spoken to Joseph Smith and practiced by members of the Church of Jesus Christ of Latter-Day Saints. Americans, busy in the transcontinental drive that caught the West up in its wake, struggled with the Mormons who were allegiant to their church.

Manifest Destiny was merciless. Not in New York, not in Missouri, not in Illinois, not in Iowa could the Mormon people stop and not be pestered. But California held promise, which was why those 238 souls boarded the *Brooklyn* in February 1846.

Some historians presume that if the Mormons who trekked out of the Midwest hadn't stopped in Utah, on land no one else wanted to claim, the Church of Jesus Christ of Latter-Day Saints might not still exist today. But in Utah, the Church and its people found some measure of peace. Now, by many accounts, the Mormon Church is growing faster than the Christian Church did in the second and third centuries.

When Church fathers called the Californians to come build their homes in the desert, some of the new immigrants traveled east across the mountains. But many of them stayed, planting the Church where they were. California now has the largest population of Mormons of any state outside of Utah. The second-largest Mormon temple outside of Utah is in Los Angeles. The sixth-largest is in Oakland.

The Oakland Temple is vast, with manicured grounds, green lawns, and lush beds of flowers. It sits one and a half miles up a hill from our apartment and has spectacular views of the entire San Francisco Bay. The sidewalk on Lincoln Avenue, leading to the temple from the valley where we live, is unbroken. A smooth path for the stroller. That sidewalk and that vantage point are the reasons I push you toward the temple on clear days.

·

YOU HAVE PERFECTED the barrel roll and now you are sitting up without assistance. Sometimes, when I need a break, I can sit you down someplace and walk a little ways away. Once sitting, you'll stay for a while, looking at books, playing with toys. Sometimes you seem a sovereign nation, my Argentina. When you cried all night in that first month, before you had a physical vocabulary for showing us your needs, I used to remind myself that one day you wouldn't want me to hold you at all, let alone for hour after hour, and then I would miss the smell of your head as it nestled all day and all night just below my chin. I knew you wouldn't be mine to hold forever, and sometimes that made me want to cry right along with you, Mourning Dove.

Today, after you called my name, I sat you in your crib where you could watch your mobile. No more *Ma Ma Ma Ma*, just a silent gaze circling with the sturdy plastic safari animals tethered over your head. That quickly, I was replaced in your attentions.

I heard a story recently about a couple who grew jealous of their daughter's mobile. They had so completely fallen in love with the way the baby gazed into their eyes that they didn't want to share her attention, even with a musical crib mobile. Irrational, yes, but something in me understands.

When the elephant passed your head for the fifteenth time, you grabbed it and went along for the ride. Your upper body followed the mobile around the crib, while your heavy, diapered bum stayed put.

It all happened quickly and slowly, so I had time to multiply into many mothers: the one who would rush toward you like a rescue team and another who would stand by the wardrobe, mouth agape, watching as, kerplop, you fell onto your back on the mattress, nearly smashing the soft part of your head on the crib slats. I had time only to think, *Oh my God oh my God oh my God*, and *That's what you get for grabbing after something that cares nothing for you*. There was humor in your predicament, but also there was the fact that your fall nearly slammed a wood bar into the anterior fontanelle where your outsized brain waits inside your as-yet-unfused skull.

How can I name what I felt when I saw you not hurt? Not this time.

Lincoln Avenue is steady and steep, and we walked up without stopping. I chose a temple viewing station, with its map and information placard, as my excuse to rest, so I was breathless when I learned about the *Brooklyn*.

I read the bronze placard, looked out over Oakland, the San Francisco Bay, Yerba Buena Island, and San Francisco. You slept in your stroller, and I watched you awhile. Then I read the placard again. I read one name and then another. A name and then an age and then another name. Your weight, and your stroller's weight, and my extra weight, I pushed all of that up Lincoln Avenue, and now there was this new weight, this old, old weight. It took my breath away.

Sarah Sloat Burr lost a boy, an unnamed one-year-old, during the voyage on the *Brooklyn*, and gave birth to another, John Atlantic. Forever after that, would she remember the dead son she shrouded and slipped into the ocean recalled by the living boy's name?

Was it meant as salt or as salve, his naming?

Jerusha H. Ensign Fowler (twenty-seven), traveling without a husband, left the East Coast with her parents, a sister, a brother, and sons ages six, five, four, and one. She arrived at Yerba Buena with no father, no sister, and no baby boy. Their bodies left behind in the water.

What mixture of celebration and mourning must have accompanied her landing?

Jane Cowen Glover brought Joseph Smith Glover (age

one) safely to California. *Relief* may not be the right word to describe her response to their arrival. When the *Brooklyn* nearly foundered in an Atlantic storm, the passengers sang hymns and prayed, assured that God would guide them safely through the voyage. Some people's prayers were answered, some of the time.

Had she not died (pregnant) on the voyage, Laura Hotchkiss Goodwin would have witnessed the safe arrival of one-year-old Albert Story Goodwin and her other children, ages three to eleven, but she died, so her seven surviving children reached Yerba Buena without a mother.

I try to imagine the lives of the women and children named on the placard.

Hard-line historical objectivists would warn against emotional anachronism. What drove these women could not be the same things that drive me today. I will allow we cannot ever wholly agree.

You cry out, my little Argentina. I pull the blanket up under your chin to protect you from the hilltop wind.

Compelled by the story revealed in the names, I read the manifest again.

•

THE HOPE THESE WOMEN had for themselves and their children's futures: Is there any other way to think of it than all-consuming? They must have been out of their minds with complicated desires. Sarah Duncan McCullough Griffith brought her two-year-old boy to California, and Caroline Augusta Perkins Joyce brought her one-year-old daughter. In addition to a five-year-old, a seven-year-old, a thirteen-year-old, and a fourteen-year-old, thirty-four-year-old Eliza Hindman Littleman boarded the *Brooklyn* with four-month-old identical twins. What was it for her to nurse those two in the ship's cramped quarters, water festering and roaches in the meal she needed to keep her milk production high? Did she feel good nursing the twins, even in the midst of that squalor?

When Octavia Anne Lane Austin left New York with children ages two, five, and seven, she couldn't have known there was gold at this end of the world. It wasn't that kind of promise that drove her to California.

Alice Wallace Bird was one month old, so she had no say in the matter. What of Ann Eliza Corwin Brannan, who had a two-month-old son? Can anyone say what it was she hungered for?

There was new life, yes, but also much common, unspeakable horror. Thirteen people died in transit. Eight of the dead were babies. Scarlet fever took the first. Consumption, diarrhea, dehydration.

Sarah Winner, six months old when the *Brooklyn* set sail, never made it to California. Oren Hopkins Smith, ten months old when the *Brooklyn* set sail, never made it to California. Mary Ann Shunn Burtis Robbins, already the mother of three children under seven, bore and buried Anna Pacific Robbins in the ocean for which she was named. When she loved her living children, did she hug them so tightly, sometimes, she nearly squeezed the life from them?

Phoebe Ann Wright Robbins (thirty-four) lost five-year-old George Edward Robbins and one-year-old John Franklin Robbins somewhere at sea. A baby, born off the West Coast of America, was a living memorial to her aunt's and mother's losses. Georgeanna Pacific Robbins. Was she salve or salt on their wounds?

·

You cry again, obviously rooting. I love that word, *rooting*. As if, by seeking your mother's milk, you are planting yourself in this world.

I take you out of the stroller and bring you with me to a bench where I can hold you while I look across the houses of Oakland and out into the Bay. You nurse while I steady my gaze on Yerba Buena Island, known in a decimated people's decimated language as Sea Bird Island.

The island was later known as Wood Island, because of sunken ships and lost treasure.

Arbor Day plantings of the nineteenth century installed invasive species that have mostly squeezed out the native plant the Spanish once called yerba buena.

I don't know what I know now that I can name these losses.

I soothe your cries and look out over the Bay toward where, sometime in 1846, Georgeanna Pacific Robbins must have cried for much the same reason and in much the same way. As she nursed her, did her mother call her darling, sweet pea, little honeybee? Georgeanna? Pacific? When she looked out at the ocean where she lost those other children, what was there to say?

I don't know if there is a name for this in any language, this hope and hurt and hunger I hold when I hold you. The story of the *Brooklyn* makes me breathless with sadness and a relief that borders on joy. *I haven't lost you yet,* I think. *I haven't lost you yet. I haven't lost you yet. Oh my God oh my God oh my God.*

BODY OF EVIDENCE

———————————

1

At the left edge of a field of ombré blue flies a rough-legged hawk, talons extended, the dark brown tips of its tail and wings unfurled, mouth open mid-key. This is the cover of my book *Smith Blue*. I loved the image from the first moment I saw it. I love the hawk's unapologetic hunger and vigor. That hunger, those talons, were nothing for which the hawk needed permission. For the cover of a book about surviving—thriving, even—in a time of global and domestic strife, Dudley Edmonson's photo of a hawk in the midst of graceful predation is perfect.

Dudley lives in Duluth. The summer my daughter turned four, my family spent a few days in northern Minnesota, aiming to take a break from the routine patterns of our lives. On our final day in the state, the three of us, plus our friend Sean Hill, drove to meet Dudley at a restaurant on the shore of Lake Superior.

As much as I liked Dudley's art, it was clear that day that my husband and Sean loved Dudley even more. The three men grew loud and large over our lunch together. They all sounded blacker to me in each other's company than they usually tended to sound. Which means that they sounded comfortable and happy in their bodies, that they cracked jokes in a particular kind of way about particular kinds of things, that they laughed upon receiving these jokes as well as on delivering them, that they danced a little when they walked. This is not to say all black people are good and constant dancers. It is to say that these three men were happy and light, that there was—as I have often heard said about others, but I have not often been able to say about my husband or these two friends—a spring in their steps.

There is a joke I have heard more than once that there are only five black birders in the country. Two of them are Sean and Dudley. Another, Drew Lanham, is also my friend. Which is to say that I am, according to lore, personally acquainted with 60 percent of the nation's black birders. And at our lunch that day, we nearly had a quorum. This would be shocking if my life weren't filled with statistics that put me in company with others who are also virtually alone.

The three men spent lunch comparing notes about living in America in black bodies that were regularly confused with the bodies of other black men. Funny at first, the stories of being mistaken for a birder half a foot taller with completely different hair. But they soon became less funny. What a menace, to live in bodies that might be anybody's, that are so frequently assumed to be corrupt. To be followed through stores by security. To be stopped and frisked as they walked to their offices. To be both erased and singled out. Their storytelling was a performance of one-upmanship. This story was worse than that story, was worse than the story one of them had just told, and always—this was the crux of the celebration, that it had not yet come to this—there was another story, much worse, that at any given moment the survivors might be left behind to tell.

After lunch, Dudley took us to one of the bluffs surrounding Lake Superior. "It was there and gone before I even saw it," he said, crouching in the spot where he'd captured our rough-legged hawk. He'd snapped the picture, but hadn't taken aim. Dudley is a masterful photographer. I am not writing this to underplay his skills. That is one of the things that keep me up at night: worrying that I'll make difficult work sound easy.

His camera, Dudley said, just happened to be pointing the right way at the right time.

2

IN THE HANS CHRISTIAN ANDERSEN story, it is the loss of her voice that does in the little mermaid. In Disney's reinvention, a sea witch draws song from Ariel's body as if her voice were a melodically manifest soul. But in the original tale, the sorceress cuts out the unnamed mermaid's tongue and throws it into a pot, the boiling contents of which sound "like the weeping of a crocodile." To lose her tail—which, among mermaids, "is considered so beautiful," but which "is thought on earth to be quite ugly"—Hans Christian Andersen's mermaid needs also to be rendered dumb. Disney maintains this element of the story, apparently conceding to the fact that fitting into the human world is a difficulty beyond words.

After she loses her voice in order to gain human legs, every step Hans Christian Andersen's mermaid takes is plagued by shooting pain, as if she were walking on knives. She'll dance anyway. She'll brave long hikes with her beloved prince—the man for whom she has determined to endure all this. Pain is a cost the little mermaid accepts for the privilege of surviving in the human world. Though, of course, she does not survive as a human. She dissolves into foam and air by the story's end.

My daughter, now five, has fallen in love with the little mermaid. Not Hans Christian Andersen's unnamed girl. Not even the Disney mermaid. I can still control what Callie watches, so she hasn't seen the Disney film with its sixteen-year-old heroine who saturated the culture's consciousness around 1989—when I was also a girl of sixteen.

What my daughter loves is the idea of a girl with a tail. Despite my attempts to keep from her both the fairy tale and the Disney movie—because I find one so sad and the other too easy—Callie has experienced enough versions of the mermaid's story to know she loves the idea of breathing underwater. She is drawn to how different mermaids' lives seem from her own. How enchanted. She likes the prospect of making a seemingly inaccessible place into her home.

Callie understands the mermaid she calls Ariel to be a fluid figure who can grow a tail or lose it on a whim. Who could blame her for coveting such transformational power? Her hero can go anywhere she wants to go. She can breathe anywhere she needs to breathe.

When I took Callie to Disneyland just after her fifth birthday, Ariel stood in a ball gown in her grotto and gave my girl a warm hug. Callie has no idea how much I paid for that privilege. Later, in the Electrical Parade, Ariel floated down Main Street waving to the crowd, tail flipping in the air. "See," Callie told me, "I told you mermaids were real." She is still young enough to believe in the impossible.

3

IN THE YEARS BEFORE HER DEATH, my maternal grandmother told me the story of her family's flight from Shreveport to Summerville, Louisiana. My great-grandfather—who owned his own sheet metal shop in that left-behind town; who could read and write and figure, and who understood his worth; who was fair enough to pass for some type of person other than a Negro; whose wife, a woman who could not pass for anything but a Negro, welcomed black and white local children into her home to teach them the civilizing art of piano-playing—entered his business one morning and found his young cousin dead on a worktable. A note pinned to the body warned my great-grandfather to get out of town by nightfall lest he be killed as well.

The surviving family piled into a wagon with nothing but what the wagon could hold. "Imagine that," my grandmother said, repeatedly, in the last years of her life. She didn't talk much about the new shop or the new town. In the years before she died, it was that wagon my grandmother talked about—loaded with what things her family could haul—and that life plucked from her family's line.

Most black American families I know have a story of some branch brutally severed from their family tree. The only remarkable thing about my grandmother's story is that she had to reach as far back as 1917 to encounter such a trauma. But pain is an immortal humor, lasting in a body far longer than pleasure. Again and again my grandmother asked me, as if I might, one visit, provide some satisfactory answer: "What would make a person do that to a body?" We might be playing with the baby, Grandmother's namesake. We might be sitting in the nursing home's courtyard, enjoying the light of the springtime sun. Once, we were in the communal dining room, surrounded by the dying old white Iowans with whom my grandparents spent their final years. She looked around, as if startled to find herself among strangers, and whispered the story of her family's flight as if it were a story that I—that moment, for my very survival— needed to hear.

Grandmother's voice shook when she recited this story. Not from age, but from a hard-driven grief that spoke through muscle to bone. This must be what they mean by visceral terror. My grandmother repeated her story because she could not help but remember. She was there. She walked into the shop and saw her cousin. (She never used his name.) She climbed into the wagon and rode through the dust. She felt her father's fear-born defiance and caution. She saw her pregnant mother, several siblings, packed up and driven off before the last of the light. She was there, you understand, and she had to tell me. Though she would likely have been too young at the time to remember the incident. This, too, is possible. Hers was the small body inside her mother's body. She might not yet have even been conceived. This is how history eclipses all reality. My grandmother, who could not help but relive this trauma, was also as far away from everything I am writing as you and as me.

4

WHEN SHE WAS FIFTEEN, my mother kept watch over her own grandmother's body. She was the eldest granddaughter, and deathwatch was her duty. She sat alone overnight in the dead woman's parlor. The coffin open before her.

My mother couldn't fathom raising children who didn't know about the fundamental trappings of death. These were, to her, part of what it meant to be alive. But she raised us in a manicured region of Southern California that tried to repudiate the existence of death. One story my mother tells is that she was driving with me down the 405 freeway near our home when we passed a hearse. I was four or five, the age my daughter is now. "What's that funny-looking car?" I asked. And because she feared for my ignorance, and because she knew what we needed to learn, mother began sending my sister and me to Chicago each summer.

There, we accompanied my grandparents on hospital visits and to funerals. We also went to weddings, and choir practice, and meetings of the women's Bible study guild. In short, we were fully involved in the life of the body of Original Providence Baptist Church.

Well after noon on those summer Sundays, if there was no luncheon planned down in the church's gym, my grandfather, the head pastor of Original Providence, would remove his clerical collar and drive a few blocks for a bucket of Church's fried chicken. We ate in his large pastoral study, on the second floor of the old stone church. My grandmother didn't cook well, and I think my grandparents, who loved language to an immoderate measure, enjoyed the pun-rich pleasure of relying on Church's after their long days at church. When we were done—let me correct that: Grandmother always said, "People are finished, cakes are done"—when the long days had finished, we drove from the West Side back through the city and around the lake to my grandparents' brick home in a South Shore neighborhood known as Pill Hill.

The Church's chicken was necessary on those long days, because my grandmother was diabetic. She always carried Brach's candy discs and kept small cartons of Tropicana in the pastoral study's fridge, but she needed regular meals. By the time she died, the pads of her fingers were so thick from recurring blood glucose tests that she had to cycle through them to give each a break. I'd watch her fold the skin and subcutaneous fat around her midsection so she could inject her insulin. "Ouch!" she'd sing, sweet as a stylish woman admitting how terribly her high heels pinched. I witnessed this ritual more often—I remember this more clearly—than hearing my grandmother, the preacher's wife, pray.

When my doctor told me that the loss of muscle function I was experiencing on one side of my face was a result of one or more lesions in my brain, he also told me that the typical protocol for treating multiple sclerosis was via an injection, and I cried. I didn't understand what it meant to have MS—I still don't understand what it means to have MS—but I understood what it meant to have to hurt yourself regularly in order to stay alive. My grandmother had diabetes. My aunt has diabetes. My mother has diabetes. Many cousins have diabetes. I have lived my life with the specter of diabetes. I understand how it works on a body. In my family, it is less a question of *if* than it is *when* the diagnosis will come. "I've spent my whole life wrestling my weight to delay the onset of diabetes," I sobbed to the doctor, "because I didn't want to have to stick a needle in myself." This sounds petulant when I write it, but I was not pouting. I had tried to stave off one of the worst things I knew, and a bad thing I'd never thought about had happened instead.

5

IN THE SOUTHEAST, trees are thick with a Southern brand of sorrow. In the Northeast, forests interrupt my sight lines. I lived on the East Coast for eleven years, and I could never fully relax. I thought the panic attacks I suffered when I wandered into the hills near the Cumberland Gap Trail had solely to do with my concern—irrational, perhaps, but irrefutable—that every rustling leaf would reveal a Confederate ghost. It was some years before I learned about epigenetics: memory retention through inherited genome. I didn't yet understand the body—or the body's DNA—as a historical ledger. In fact, we are only now beginning to understand the implications of epigenetics. I do know that the experiences of the people whose bodies went into making my body must live in me—their lives shadowing my life, like ghosts.

I prefer hiking in the West to hiking in the East.

I'm not saying there are no ghosts in California. Ray and I once hiked with the baby up a slope that for more than three thousand years hosted some of the largest trees on Earth. The mother trees have been logged, but rings of younger trees—some call them fairy rings—circle the sites where those giants once reigned.

Fairy rings can measure as much as fifty feet in diameter, a circle of new growth over a hundred years old. We tried to show the baby how big one mother tree must have been, but she picked up a small rock and threw it away. Then she picked up another rock and threw it, also, away. She was two and a half. Everything around her was older and taller and larger than she. The horrible violence we had visited on this landscape—and the ways that the landscape corrected the trauma—were of no consequence to my little girl.

Our family circled the huddle of second-growth trees. Callie picked up a pebble and threw it, some distance, away.

6

SOMETIMES, WHEN I AM WORKING on moving words around a page, doing exactly what I most love, I think of my grandmothers, their husbands, their parents, and their parents as well. Every one of my grandparents had at least a college education. All of my mother's grandparents had college educations, and three of her grandparents had master's degrees, too. My father's mother earned her RN in 1929. Because she was black and a woman and could not attend nursing school in her home state, she traveled from Illinois to New York for the privilege. My mother's mother died with a doctorate. My mother's father died with two doctoral degrees, the first of which he completed at Columbia University because none of his of own state's institutions would admit a black man. When my mother told her father she wanted to study art in college, her father insisted she obtain a practical degree instead. (She majored in political science and minored in history.) When I say I feel guilty when I could be writing and I am not writing, it is with this background in the foreground. If I am wasting time, it is not my time alone I have squandered. I don't feel selfish when I focus my attention on writing because, when I am writing well, I am never writing my story alone.

I am conscious always of these disparate, powerful influences—though they might bind my story together, they also might tear me apart.

When I am writing, it is always about history. What else could I be writing about? History is the synthesis of our lives.

7

AN ISSUE OF *Ebony* magazine published after Ronald Reagan's 1981 inauguration expresses concerns over what the election of this new president would mean for black Americans: "When Ronald Reagan was swept into the White House by a landslide vote, no one was more affected than the many Blacks who were brought into the government by the administration of Jimmy Carter, a president who had set an all-time record for the number of top government jobs awarded to Blacks and the number of [black] guests invited to White House functions. Blacks supported Carter almost 90 percent but Reagan won." Such an enactment of estrangement, to live in a country where the vote of 90 percent of your community has no practical effect.

I was the only person in my second-grade class who voted for Jimmy Carter. April Lewis, the other black girl in the class, did not participate in our grade's mock election. She was a Jehovah's Witness, and Jehovah's Witnesses, because their law is of a higher order, are not encouraged to vote.

I knew this about April and the Jehovah's Witnesses not because April and I were close—we were not close—but because April's grandmother, Mrs. Lewis, welcomed me home every afternoon when I returned from school, so that I would not have to be alone.

Mrs. Lewis was our babysitter and housekeeper. She was from someplace in the South like Oklahoma—a part of the South that was still Southern, but seemed to me less deeply so—and she cooked the only fried chicken and lima beans I have ever truly loved. Her beans were buttery and so delicious that, even in those years when "lima beans" were words children used to mean "torture," I ate two or three servings every time Mrs. Lewis spooned them onto my plate.

On school nights when my parents worked late, or on weekends when they went off to black-tie galas for the Urban League or the Links, Inc., Mrs. Lewis fed us and made sure we were tucked safely into bed. I loved Mrs. Lewis. I loved the kind of clean she kept our kitchen, family room, living room. I loved her in a way that was as deeply complicated and uncomplicated as constructs of social class and race. I loved Mrs. Lewis like the grandmother she was, despite all the evidence to prove we were not from the same family. What we relate to and whom, I learned in those years, stems from connections—and divisions—that are often heedless of blood. By blood, I mean both kinship and the stuff that flows from our wounds.

Connecting with one group often requires separation from others. One of the ways that Reagan won the 1980 election was by activating a strong base of a certain type of voter. He kicked off his campaign by giving a speech at the Neshoba County Fair, a site just outside of Philadelphia, Mississippi. Nearby, just sixteen years before Reagan's speech, the young Freedom Riders James Chaney, Andrew Goodman, and Michael Schwerner were murdered. Reagan apologists remind us that plenty of candidates held major campaign events at the Neshoba County Fair, which reminds me that plenty of candidates are unconcerned with the traumas recalled by the site.

On the campaign trail, Reagan opposed the Voting Rights Act of 1965 and the Civil Rights Act of 1964—acts that the murder of Chaney, Goodman, and Schwerner helped to propel. In his Neshoba County Fair speech, Reagan spoke to the crowd about his support of "states' rights," a coinage designed to attract a pro-segregationist audience.

While running for governor of California in 1966, Ronald Reagan vowed to help eradicate the Rumford Act, legislation passed in 1963 that banned discrimination with regard to financial transactions related to housing. In his opposition of the Act, Reagan said, "If an individual wants to discriminate against Negroes or others in selling or renting his house, it is his right to do so." The Rumford Act was supported by the California Supreme Court and the United States Supreme Court, but Reagan continued to oppose it until the Federal Fair Housing Act of 1968 rendered his efforts irrelevant. Perhaps his defeat on this front was part of why he believed that legislation like the Voting Rights Act of 1965 was "humiliating to the South." When he spoke about the South and the rights of an individual in such cases, Reagan was not speaking about individuals like my great-grandparents, my grandparents, Mrs. Lewis, my parents, or me. Even at seven years old, making sense of the political climate around me, I understood the rhetoric of exclusion.

My parents were not quiet about their thoughts on Reagan. They discussed politics over dinner, talked back to NPR and the television news. Before I was born, I learned, while my father earned his master's in public health from Johns Hopkins University, my parents lived in Baltimore. Mother looked for an apartment when they arrived, calling in response to a listing, hearing there was a lovely unit available, and arriving in her black body to discover the unit had just been rented to someone else. Or that there never was a unit available, my mother must have had the wrong address. Or that the landlord had changed her mind about renting the apartment after all. My parents sued the city of Baltimore for housing discrimination. But they were young, my father was completing his medical training, and they didn't have the money or time to see the case through. They left Baltimore—couldn't get out quickly enough, my mother says—lived for a few years in Colorado, then moved to California, where Governor Reagan had worked hard to reverse legislation aimed at reducing housing discrimination.

When people ask what it was like to grow up black in Irvine, California, in the seventies and eighties, I tell them the story of being the only person in my class to cast a vote for Jimmy Carter. The rest of my class, the rest of my county, the rest of my country—they all voted for the other candidate in a landslide. A candidate to whom—I must have understood this even as a child—my family's voice, our pain, meant little.

It was just a mock election, the second-grade teachers said. It didn't really matter.

8

IT WAS IN THE FALL OF 2013, a few months after I relocated my family to Colorado, that half of my face stopped moving.

I didn't have Bell's palsy, my Internet research told me, because the part of my face I couldn't control was pulled upward, not downward. My cheek did not droop. Rather, it was plumped up. One eye was nearly closed as a result of the up-pull on that cheek. To balance the look, I went through my days with a forced expression of joy. I was newly acquainting myself with my colleagues and students, the parents of my daughter's new classmates, my neighbors, and I smiled all day and all night. I didn't feel like engaging this new community in speculation about what might be happening to my body, so I smiled through classes. I smiled through meetings. I smiled at day-care pickup and at the new grocery store.

Some facts are depressing, but that doesn't mean I don't want to know. My new town had about 156,000 people, 1.2 percent of whom were defined by the U.S. Census Bureau's Quick Facts sheet as "Black or African American alone." By this, they meant people who did not identify as multiracial. But in my case, the phrase seemed painfully accurate. As a black faculty member of my department, I was alone. I was alone as a black female faculty member of the College of Liberal Arts at my new university. The only one. I was—this fact is astonishing every time I encounter it—virtually alone as a black faculty member of the entire university. Of 1,045 tenured and nontenured professors employed that year, only eleven of us were black. And it wasn't like I could go someplace else and find things radically different. In the entire United States I was one of fewer than fifteen African American female full professors teaching in my field. The number was actually twelve, but I liked to say "fewer than fifteen" in the hopes that I might have neglected to count someone. I kept track of these facts because they confirmed what I already knew. I was as inconceivable as any mermaid, making a place for myself in my new home.

One of the prime symptoms of multiple sclerosis is extreme and sustained exhaustion. Neural damage affects the nerves' myelin sheath and hinders the nerves' abilities to send messages between the brain and the body. I am, in this way, always at risk of being disconnected from myself. Researchers presume that compensating for this disruption is a large part of what causes the chronic fatigue experienced by MS patients.

It took a while to find a clinic that would accept me as a new patient. While I waited for an appointment with a doctor, and when I wasn't knocked out from sheer exhaustion, I made myself smile.

9

DUDLEY AND HIS WIFE, Nancy, were going to lead us partway to scenic Two Harbors the day my family went with Sean Hill to Duluth, but a few miles up the road, they switched on their indicator and we pulled off at a lakeside turnout. Dudley hopped out of his car and ran back to tell us that they'd had so much fun with us they'd decided to change their plans so they could come hear the poetry reading Sean was scheduled to deliver later that afternoon. "It's not often," he said, "we get to hang out with people we have so much in common with."

We decided to park the cars, and then we scrabbled down an embankment. Callie touched the water of a lake so large it could flood both North and South America in a foot of water. I held on to her, a little afraid of the basin that holds 10 percent of all the world's fresh surface water. The pebbles and rocks Callie threw created tiny ripples. We watched them awhile, and then climbed into our cars to see more of Duluth.

What seeing more of Duluth included was visiting the site of a lynching.

"You wrote about a lynching that happened in your hometown," Dudley told Sean after the reading. "I want to take you up the street to show you the memorial to a lynching that happened here." We are all telling the same story. When writing about race, there can perhaps be precious little wholly fresh revelation. As with writing about motherhood. It has been the same story for as long as anyone can remember. As with writing about the corruption of the body. As with writing about the landscapes of our world.

We walked up a hill and looked toward the corner of First Street and Second Avenue. From a streetlight there, ninety-four years and fourteen days earlier, hung the mutilated bodies of Elias Clayton, Elmer Jackson, and Isaac McGhie. For the sculptures erected to memorialize the three, artist Carla Stetson used young local men as models.

This is where I am supposed to tell you the story behind the lynching of Clayton, Jackson, and McGhie, but there really isn't any reason for it. Clayton, Jackson, and McGhie were black bodies in the wrong place at the wrong time—which could be any place in this country, at any time.

Roustabout is one of the words used to describe Clayton, Jackson, and McGhie, which meant they worked for the John Robinson Circus as cooks and physical laborers. Consider *outlandish*: people—originally black people—who come from other places and bring with them "outlandish" ways of moving through the world. Consider *hippie*: in the Senegambian language known as Wolof, "hippi"—from which we get the terms *hip, hippie,* and *hipster*—means to open one's eyes. And also *to be sold downriver*: a phrase that originally referred to the sale of enslaved human beings to more treacherous destinations along the Mississippi River basin. Words with derogatory shading—like *roustabout*—are often words that were associated with black bodies as they moved through America.

These particular roustabouts happened to be working in a circus that visited Duluth. On June 15, 1920, a mob of white men—some say more than a thousand, while others say as many as ten thousand—wanted them dead. The three men were being held in jail, supposedly for their protection. "The people who were outside were saying, 'Just give us somebody,' and that first somebody was a young man named Isaac McGhie," says Michael Fedo, author of the book *The Lynchings in Duluth*.

The last sentence on the Clayton Jackson McGhie Memorial reads, "This memorial is dedicated to the memories of the murdered here and everywhere." Our little party spent a good deal of time walking around the monument. It fills a whole corner of the block and features quotations by people like James Baldwin, Martin Luther King, Jr., and Euripides. "The truth is rarely pure, and never simple," Oscar Wilde. "The world is a dangerous place, not because of those who do evil, but because of those who look on and do nothing," Albert Einstein. Siddhartha Guatama: "Holding onto anger is like grasping a hot coal with the intent of throwing it at someone else. You are the one getting burned." Over the top of the monument scrolls a quote from Edmund Burke: "An event has happened upon which it is difficult to speak and impossible to remain silent." The quotations are familiar. If not in their particulars, at least in their ilk. Written against the damage we do to others and ourselves. The only new language is the description of the final hours of the lives of Clayton, Jackson, and McGhie.

I pointed my camera catty-corner across the street to the site where McGhie, Jackson, and Clayton were killed. (I keep using their names because I don't want to let myself be part of the men's erasure.) Duluth has maintained its brick streets in this section of town, but in places, as in the intersection of First Street and Second Avenue, there are tarred spots to patch potholes. My photo also reveals a crack in the sidewalk leading toward Second Avenue. The harsh climate in Duluth takes its toll.

In the image, the streetlight on that particular corner was attached to an arm from which hung a number of signs. The first sign read FIRST ST. The second was gray with a white P in a blue circle. PUBLIC PARKING, it read. A white arrow indicated which direction to proceed. The final sign, closest to the traffic light— which was red in my photo—was black-and-white. It read ONE WAY. An arrow pointed in the direction of the Clayton Jackson McGhie Memorial. Sometimes it is easy to draw meaning from the arbitrary order of things.

Ray's arms are long, and so it was he who captured a photograph of all of us in front of the monument. My four-year-old daughter, three of my favorite black men, Nancy, and me.

10

Factors that have been proven not to cause multiple sclerosis: environmental allergies, living with a dog, aspartame, physical trauma.

A history of smoking may predispose a person to developing MS. A diagnosis of migraine, which I also have, is coincident in one-third of patients diagnosed with MS. Exposure to heavy metals does not predispose a person to developing MS. There is no word yet on why one person may and another may not develop MS. Factors that are coincident are not necessarily causal.

Disease progression for relapsing-remitting multiple sclerosis (the version of the disease with which I have been diagnosed) varies, but "is characterized by clearly defined attacks of new or increasing neurologic symptoms." This is what the National Multiple Sclerosis Society website tells me. A close friend, whose mother died from MS last month, tells me it is a horrible way to die. But the National Multiple Sclerosis Society website tells me that people don't actually die from MS. They die from complications caused by MS. The loss of the ability to swallow. Infections caused by the inability to clear the bladder. Falls caused by the inability to control spasticity. And while we are living, which is also while we are dying, neuropathy may provoke the sensation of walking on stilettos—by which I mean the feeling of walking on knives.

The second identified manifestation of my multiple sclerosis initially presented itself well before I was diagnosed with the disease. This is what it is like for many of us. We search through our personal histories to discover all the instances when damage to our nervous systems might have occurred.

In the last months of my pregnancy and after my daughter's difficult delivery, I had to hold banisters to walk safely down stairs. This was, I assumed, because of the baby. My feet grew half a size, my bras were radically different, essentially everything I'd come to know about myself over thirty-seven years had changed. But my optometrist assured me that my eyesight should return to normal eventually. By normal, she meant I would eventually go back to seeing the world the way I saw things before I became a mother. This has not yet transpired.

Everyone in my family wears glasses. I thought the challenges with my vision were an extension of my family's reality. I resigned myself to living with compromised depth perception. At the end of a day, I'd stall on the BART platform—adjusting my computer bag while commuters scurried down to the exit—because stepping onto crowded escalators filled me with a tumbling fear.

During the inaugural celebration for her husband's second term, I watched Michelle Obama walk down the Capitol steps wearing knee-high black suede boots with kitten heels. *I'd be afraid of falling*, I thought in awe. This wasn't a political statement.

The underlying issue, finally diagnosed in the summer of

2013, is called diplopia. I have difficulty correcting vertical disjunctions. One world, seen through one eye, is always a little bit on top of the other, and my eyes and brain exhaust themselves making sense of these discrepancies.

It was two more years before a new eye doctor suggested that the condition might be linked to my recently diagnosed MS. Diplopia turns out to be a relatively common secondary condition that manifests when MS lesions develop where several of my lesions have left scars.

Multiple sclerosis is not heritable, but having someone in your immediate family with MS does increase the likelihood of developing MS. Nobody in my immediate family has MS. Now I am the link between the disease and any person—I worry about my daughter—who is implicated by my medical history. I asked my neurologist if he knew why I might have developed MS, and he said that no one has a clear answer for these kinds of things.

Being of African, or Asian, or Native American descent may mean you are at lower risk of developing MS, but that didn't help me. Being a woman instead of a man may change the way my body will suffer. But it may have no bearing at all. Reduced vitamin D levels may predispose a person to developing MS. Living in a temperate climate may increase the risk of developing MS. Living in the Northern Hemisphere in the years after puberty may predispose a person to developing MS. In other words, growing into adulthood in America may predispose a person to this chronic disease.

Some people go years without knowing they have MS—as I did. Some people have MS and pass through life in such a manner that you would not know they have the disease—as I basically do. Sometimes the brain works around neural damage, so that a body seems to behave just as it did before any damage occurred—as my body seems to be doing. I can't assume it will always be this way for me. Living, now, in this body, I have to grow used to the possibility of the worst outcome manifesting at any time. For the time being, what I do is swallow a tasteless pill twice a day. Sometimes radical self-care can be as painless as that. I have come to understand MS as a fact of my life, like my race, my gender, the fact I'm Callie's mother: something fundamental that both does and does not change anything—everything—about the way I move through the world.

11

I'VE HAD TO LEARN about all kinds of things that may or may not help the survival of living beings in general and my family in particular. For instance, some 85 to 95 percent of people are sensitive to urushiol—the reactive agent in western poison oak. It is thought that bathing in hot water can increase the severity of a systemic reaction to urushiol, but that washing with cold water and one of a number of specialized soaps can avert the onset of a systemic response. If all else fails, a person may mitigate the power of the oil by rubbing exposed skin with uncompromised dirt.

Western poison oak was not much of a problem when it was first identified in 1830 by the same David Douglas who identified a prominent western tree now called the Douglas fir. But western poison oak thrives on disruption, so the Gold Rush and the silver rush and the timber rush and the housing development rush that made California the California that we now know facilitated the spread of *Toxicodendron diversilobum*. When you hike in California, as I enjoy doing, you should be mindful of western poison oak.

"Don't touch that," I told Ray and Callie, pointing out the red-tinged, three-leafed menace. Along the trails in the hills near our old Oakland apartment, western poison oak grew thick. Ray wanted to know why poison oak is tinged red, and I said the same was often true with poison ivy; that I didn't know if it was true for poison sumac; that those were the three plants in the continental United States that we typically worry about in terms of topical poison; that I didn't actually know where poison sumac grew, but that we could look it up when we arrived home; that you'll usually break out in an uncomfortable rash if you are sensitive to and touch poison oak; that repeated exposure can make reactions worse; but that I knew people who ate honey sourced from poison oak to reduce their histaminic reactions. We were walking toward the car, nearly at the end of the trail. This was one of the last hikes we would take in these hills before we moved to Colorado and I'd have to learn a whole new set of things to warn my family about.

"So that's poison oak?" asked Ray. But it wasn't. Blackberry bushes, I said, often look like poison oak, and the two plants frequently grow near each other. I told him what a good mimic poison oak was, blending in with the plants around it. The *diversilobum* part of the plant's binomial had to do with the many guises it could take—sometimes a shrub, sometimes a vine, sometimes a ground cover, sometimes like a tree. Sometimes three-leafed, sometimes as many as five or seven leaves on a stem. The leaves of *Toxicodendron diversilobum* might appear lobed, scalloped, or toothed, I said. Their colors shifted. Their size.

High levels of phosphorus, calcium, and sulfur make poison oak leaves a desirable food source for black-tailed deer. Black bears, muskrats, and pocket mice also eat the leaves and stems, while scores of California's birds rely on its seeds and berries. Sparrows use it for shelter from hawks, the California towhee and the endangered least Bell's vireo build nests in its cover, and the western pond turtle seeks shelter in patches of poison oak when the rivers flood. The California landscape would be quite different—its diversity likely radically depleted—without western poison oak. Beetles, hairstreak butterflies, native and European honeybees, crane flies, cellophane bees, mining bees, and moths pollinate the plant. The plant helps ecosystems recover after disruptions like fires, hosting larvae and small creatures all the while. Poison oak is beloved among most every living thing (except humans), but it was probably safest, I told my husband, to avoid touching anything he suspected might do him harm.

Several strides ahead, Callie turned to face us, her hands full of toxic leaves. "This, Mama? Don't touch this?"

I stopped, unsure if I could protect her. Or if I was already too late.

12

THAT NIGHT IN DULUTH, dinner turned into a lingering dessert. The restaurant closed around us. Callie fell asleep with her head in my lap.

Our family had to fly back to Colorado early the next day. In the front seat of the car, Sean and Ray kept up their conversation after we finally said goodbye to Dudley. The two-lane highway was dark. Callie and I tried to doze in the backseat's blackness. Ray passed two sedans, pulling into the lead like a speed racer.

Lights and a siren filled our car.

When the Minnesota State Patrol officer approached the passenger-side window, he found two black men prepared for the worst. Sean's hands were open and positioned on the dashboard. Ray's arms were in the air, the wallet in his hand already open to his ID. Long before he met me, Ray attended police academy in California. There are over a thousand code violations you can come up with, he told me. If you want to pull someone over, he told me, you can always come up with a reason. He told me this when we were driving in our new town in Colorado and, for no apparent reason, he was pulled over. I asked, What were you doing wrong? This, he reminded me, is an irrelevant question.

"Uh, sir," said the officer, clearly startled by the two black men in their positions of surrender, "you can put your hands down."

Ray did so, but very slowly, handing his ID to the officer as part of the arc. The cop, after trying to strike a balance between reassuring him and scolding him for speeding, walked to the squad car and ran the license numbers to see if there were warrants in

Ray's name. Mosquitoes swarmed through the open window as the officer handed Ray his citation. I slowly covered my daughter's exposed skin with a light sweater, trying not to alarm anyone with a sudden slap.

I'd been in Minnesota the year before to teach at the same writers' conference that had brought my family to the state that summer. The day I flew in the first time, self-appointed neighborhood watchman George Zimmerman was acquitted of the murder of Trayvon Martin, a seventeen-year-old black kid walking home from buying snacks. Our routine traffic stop happened just a week after Texas police shot and killed thirty-eight-year-old Jason Harrison, a black man. And one month earlier, Eric Garner, a black forty-three-year-old father of six, was choked to death by New York Police Department officers. It was six weeks before Ferguson police shot Michael Brown, and five months before Cleveland police shot and killed twelve-year-old Tamir Rice while he played in a community recreation center. I made it clear to Callie that she should not, for the meantime, open her mouth to ask what was going on.

Nine months before we were pulled over, unarmed twenty-four-year-old Jonathan Ferrell endured and died from ten gunshot wounds when he approached police officers while seeking help after a car accident. Moses Wilson, one of the jurors who sought a murder conviction for the police officer who shot Ferrell, said after the trial, "It became not what he did, or what they did to him, but more, what he didn't do, what he should have known what to do, so that the police would not either beat him silly or shoot him." These are some of the reasons that Sean's hands remained on the dashboard when we were pulled over.

Sandra Bland had not yet been killed after a routine traffic stop in Waller County, Texas, but in June 2012, the unarmed twenty-three-year-old Shantel Davis had been shot by police just after shouting, "I don't want to be killed, don't kill me!" In a month, Renisha McBride would be shot in the head when she knocked on a door seeking help after a car accident in Dearborn Heights, Michigan. Racial profiling proved fatal again. I wish I could say that the night my family sat on the side of the road in Minnesota I couldn't have imagined that two years later, just thirty minutes from the airport we would use to fly out of the state the next day, four-year-old Dee'Anna Reynolds would find herself trying to console her mother from the backseat of a car whose driver, Philando Castile, had just been shot and killed by a panicked police officer. But I worry about such horrors all the time. These incidents, those that happened before and those that would happen later—like the monument we'd visited earlier that afternoon—were not irrelevant to our behavior that evening.

The four of us had no voices as we pulled back onto the highway and drove north through the pitch-black night.

After a few miles, Ray laughed, breaking our silence. "One thing we can say for sure," he said into the darkness, remembering the officer's shocked expression when we rolled down the window and he took us all in. "That was *not* a case of driving while black."

These are the jokes you make when you are always, at some level, afraid for your life.

13

"You've got to read this *New Yorker* article about inequality," said a woman who shared a kitchen with me in April 2014.

"No. I don't."

"Oh, but you must," said she.

"I already know about inequality," I said.

We were both beneficiaries of enormous wealth and generosity, living on a billionaire's 584-acre California ranch for a month while we wrote. Rolling hills, second-growth redwoods, a groundskeeper who cut back the poison oak. No other houses in sight.

I used to do this sort of thing all the time, but I'd married and had a child. This was the first time since my daughter's birth that I'd been able to attend an artists' retreat where I could focus on nothing but my own writing. I published four books between 2009 and 2011, but I'd taken on more teaching obligations in order to support my family, and I was nowhere near completing anything new. When I'd accepted the invitation to attend this residency, it was because I would be relatively close to our Oakland apartment. I figured I could drop everything and drive home if anyone needed me. I could live the life of an artist, I thought, but not at my family's expense.

This artist residency was eight miles from my favorite beach—the beach I used to visit when I was a student at Stanford. After difficult days, my younger self would drive to that beach to walk among traces of sea foam. Once, while we were at the colony, several of the artists took a trip down to the water's edge I knew and loved, but because I was away from home to work, not to cavort at the shoreline, during the rest of my residency I had to be satisfied with the view from our high point in the Coast Range. On clear days, I could see the point break.

Our benefactor's wife, before she died of cancer, had been one of my most beloved professors. He visited the retreat's common area one day, and he and I spoke of her with the measured fondness of people who knew more about a person than a eulogy will reveal. Our disparate histories merged for the time it took to recollect the dead woman's life.

My fellow colony guests would get a chance to sit with him, but for a time I monopolized our host. When he was a boy of sixteen—a Jewish immigrant from Vienna—he'd written a letter to Eleanor Roosevelt. "I need a scholarship," he'd written. According to the portion of his narrative in which I was most deeply invested, the opportunity to attend an American university set him on the path to success.

My own grandfather—no less bold, though slightly older, having already graduated from Southern University with honors— had written his own letter to the president's wife around the same time. He was about to leave Louisiana to attend Oberlin Seminary in Ohio, my grandfather had informed Mrs. Roosevelt. None of the scholarship-granting bodies to which he'd applied were willing to give money to a black student. This was 1939. He asked her, what was a young man interested in his own education to do?

Each year, Mrs. Roosevelt sent enough money to cover my grandfather's education expenses, plus a little extra for an overcoat.

In his colony's common area, I asked my host how frequently

young men had written Mrs. Roosevelt with requests such as these. Until I'd read this other account—a proud point in many interviews—my mother's father was the only such person I knew. I was excited to share my grandfather's story with him, but my host was less pleased than I'd expected. "I thought I was the only one," he said. He turned away from me, body posture suggesting he didn't like the idea of my grandfather's history overshadowing his own. He was an old man now, and for all those years I imagine he'd cherished the belief that Mrs. Roosevelt's largesse had been for his benefit alone.

"It's a fascinating article," persisted the writer with whom I was sharing the colony's kitchen. "The author, a Harvard economist, shows how inequality really does happen."

"I'm so pleased," I said, "to know a Harvard economist has an opportunity to demonstrate to *New Yorker* readers what I have always known." We'd lived in a densely populated part of Northern California, fifty miles from the billionaire's property; but when my husband finished his Ph.D. and still couldn't find work for nearly half a decade, we had to leave the state.

"Oh, yes, of course." She was chastened. "We've been talking about this for fifteen or twenty years."

"Fifteen or twenty? Try four hundred, or more."

"Oh," she said, "aren't you ironic."

14

Five houses into our Colorado real estate tour, my husband and I stepped into the house that became our home. I loved it on sight. When we brought our daughter to visit the house, she made gleeful snow angels on the living room carpet. Ray walked down the street to get a sense of the neighborhood, something he'd done at no other house on our tour. While I stood on the porch looking after him, an elderly white woman strolled by. I worried that she might call the owners and warn them that black people were looking at their property. But the sale went through without a hitch.

After several months, I realized that I loved our house because it could have been a sibling of the Irvine house I'd once called home. The house where Mrs. Lewis was waiting for me when I came in from school. The only house, despite all the houses in which I've slept, about which I still regularly dream. Moving into this new house, I realized, was a way to unite parts of myself that had existed independently all this time. It was, I now understand, a way to put around my family a structure that might help me to feel like I belonged to someplace safe.

On the stairwell that looks out over our new living room, I hung my favorite image of my family of origin. I am five, and I am positioned in the highest spot, one hand on my hip, balanced in the nook of a shaggy eucalyptus. I am wearing a confident smile, Afro puffs, and a white cotton sundress with thick straps, red piping, and appliquéd flowers. A thin red ribbon cinches my waist. Callie wore the dress—my mother saved it—to her third day of kindergarten, but the Colorado cold came on too fast for me to take the photograph I wanted, posed as in this 1977 family portrait. This time, Callie would be in my position and I would stand in my mother's, which, so frequently now, is how my life looks to me—Callie's life repeating my life, which repeats the lives before mine.

Around the second anniversary of our move, we watched a super moon undergo a total eclipse. I tried to understand what was happening well enough to articulate the process to Callie, who watched with our new neighbors in the cul-de-sac. The Earth, I explained, in its orbit around the sun, occasionally lines up in front of the moon as it orbits the Earth, blocking the moon's direct access to sunlight. I could tell it was difficult for her to comprehend the causes and the effects of this overshadowing. Soon she would grow too autonomous for me to use her body for such lessons, but that night I placed her little hand behind my larger hand, then passed my other hand, acting as our world, between the two. Instead of sunlight reflected off the face of the moon, I showed her, we were seeing the Earth's shadow and the glow of whatever light managed to make it around us.

A neighbor came out with a pair of binoculars, and each of us took a turn pointing them in the direction of the lunar event. Someone remarked on how much rounder the moon looked that night, its contours heightened by the eclipse. One of us said it looked like an actual sphere—meaning it looked more real at that moment than it normally does. In our shadow, the moon seemed like a hunk of rock in which we could believe. I mean the moon, which we knew was a quarter of a million miles away from the spot where we stood, and which was, therefore, too distant for us to truly take in, seemed closer, more tangible, at the height of the eclipse. From our vantage point down in the cul-de-sac, the moon appeared to be a rich and lovely brown.

We were seeing, when we looked at it this way, the power—and the limits—of a shadow.

INHERENT RISK, OR WHAT I
KNOW ABOUT INVESTMENT

On Balancing a Career, a Child, and Creative Writing

"Back in our day, our children were the center of our lives," Mother said. "It seems like it's so different for your generation. You just keep doing what you were doing before the baby arrived. It's amazing to me."

This was the third week of the spring semester, eight months after Callie's birth. I was in the backseat of my parents' car, next to the baby, on the way to my office. I'd just described my upcoming spring schedule as my father drove us over the San Francisco–Oakland Bay Bridge, through the heart of the city, past the boisterous neighborhood of my single days, through the working-class residential neighborhoods I'd never visited, and on to the San Francisco State University campus. My parents were going to spend the day taking care of their grandchild. I would teach late into the evening.

After a decade living away from California, I'd been back in the Bay Area for four years and hoped I could be there for good. That spring, I was under review for tenure and promotion. New baby or not, I needed to perform. ▪

Mondays and Tuesdays that semester, I'd teach my full load of three, three-hour creative writing seminars. I would meet with students about their theses and writing projects, schedule advising meetings, wait in my office during the institutionally required office hours, attend committee meetings about college-wide paper use and office supply rations, and sit through departmental meetings about how to manage budget cuts and curriculum changes. I'd leave for campus at eight a.m. Monday and arrive home around eleven p.m., and I'd be back out of the house from nine a.m. until nine p.m. Tuesday. Then, with papers to grade and classes to prep, I'd board a plane to give lectures at colleges across the country. First there would

---

Risk and Investment

When he built the Palace Hotel in 1875 at the corner of Market and New Montgomery, William C. Ralston, cofounder of the Bank of California, insured his San Francisco marvel against destruction. Walls twelve feet thick at the foundation, the rigging a crisscross of iron, he constructed the seven-story Palace of marble, brick, cement, and stone. Hoarding 760,000 gallons of water, rooftop tanks and underground reservoirs protected the hotel. The building fared well through the 1906 earthquake. But because its water reserves were depleted in an attempt to spare neighboring buildings in the subsequent fire, the Palace could not save itself.

---

be Fort Kent, Maine; then Pittsburgh; then Cedar Rapids; then Austin. Between cities, I'd come home, teach, then get back on the road again. ▪

I traveled two to three times a month for these gigs. The salary I made teaching and the extra money I made as a visiting writer supported us.

My husband couldn't accompany Callie and me on our trips or take long hours away from writing to watch the baby while I was teaching. When we'd met, Ray was working on the first draft of his dissertation. He'd take bits of time away from writing and teaching adjunct classes to court me, but then he'd get right back to work.

When we were dating, I made him sandwiches and stock-piled lasagnas in his freezer so he could focus. I wanted him to concentrate on completing his Ph.D., not on making lunches. Once, we took a three-day road trip to the Port Townsend Writers' Conference in Washington State, where I was scheduled to teach a workshop. That drive was our first vacation together, his only vacation for ages, but once he dropped me off, he drove

---

Home

The Peralta Land Grant, the Rancho San Antonio, once constituted approximately 112 square miles and encompassed what would become the cities of Albany, Berkeley, Emeryville, Oakland, Piedmont, and San Leandro. A stretch of land my family now called home. Given to Don Luis María Peralta in recognition of his forty years of service to the Crown of Spain, the estate was worth more than $1 million when Peralta died in 1851. Don Luis and his sons could ride out and map their territory every day for a year and still not cover all of it.

---

the thirteen hours home—nonstop—so he could return to his dissertation. ▪

After we were married, and I was, to borrow a coinage shared with me by a transplant from the Ozarks, "with squirrel," Ray and I decided he would stop teaching adjunct courses so he could focus on finishing his dissertation and thus be more immediately in the position to land a proper-paying job. Our growing family would need two secure incomes but, for now, completing the dissertation had to be his full-time job or the years he'd already invested at the University of Chicago would be, in a substantial way, for naught.

The big worry was who would take care of our child while I worked and Ray wrote. My parents were only visiting for two more weeks. Once the semester started in earnest, we'd be on our own. Most day-care centers' hours didn't align with our quirky schedules. Quality nannies in the Bay Area cost between $3,000

Home Again

Most of the time I forget that all this land once belonged to a single family: the Peraltas. In 1847, there weren't more than 160,000 people in all of the California Territory. On Rancho San Antonio, there were as many as eight thousand head of cattle, two thousand horses, sixteen houses, and a wharf. The Peraltas commanded conscripted Indian laborers, and Spanish laborers, too. Peralta told the four sons who would inherit his estate, "This land is our gold." In the summer, after the rains had passed and the grasses on the hills that ringed the ranchero returned to dormancy, everywhere the brothers looked they must have seen this gold. But by the 1970s, a hundred years after the death of the last son, even the house he died in had been subdivided into low-rent apartments for newcomers to the state.

---

and $4,000 a month, a salary far surpassing what Ray made as an adjunct lecturer and approaching my post-tax income. It would be prohibitively expensive to arrange around-the-clock home child care. We could no more fit a live-in nanny into our budget than we could accommodate one in our twelve-hundred-square-foot rented apartment.

Hiring full-time help was out of the question, but so was delaying Ray's dissertation any longer or my working less. Our challenge, like that of so many new parents, was to find a workable solution that fit somewhere between these extremes.

I hoped to nurse Callie through her second birthday, and my long trips away would make that logistically difficult unless I kept her with me. Until she turned two, she could fly with me for free, as a lap child. Considering all these factors, Ray and I decided it made economic, emotional, and developmental sense for her to come along on my visiting writer gigs, and we established piecemeal solutions for my long days on campus. ▪

These gigs were a welcome opportunity, both financially and professionally. As California suffered one budget crisis after another, my salary, tied to a state-run education system, had

---

Structural Solutions

The sturdy base that supported San Francisco's Transamerica Pyramid through the 1989 Loma Prieta earthquake was built on the site of the old Montgomery Block, a massive brick building constructed in 1853 over the buried debris that helped to make a bay into a port, and a port into a landfill, and a landfill into a market center and then an artists' enclave and finally the financial center of one of the largest cities in the modern West.

---

been chipped away by furloughs and freezes. Money grew tighter just as our family grew larger. Even if the state recovered from its most recent financial woes, there would likely be more down the line. Not accepting invitations for speaking engagements wasn't realistic. The influx of cash these appearances provided came like the sort of gift that a great-aunt stipulates you spend on socks and healthy food. ∎

"I just can't imagine doing all that traveling with a baby," said Mother.

I didn't want to imagine not doing it.

This book tour wasn't just about the money. I'd had a baby. I was now a mother and a wife. In my mind that meant something separate, meant I'd become someone separate, from the person who wrote books.

In the months before Callie was born, I published the anthologies *Black Nature* and *From the Fishouse* and also my own second book, *Suck on the Marrow*. *Smith Blue*—the sixth

---

Money

A. P. Giannini, whose Genoese father had found fortune in the goldfields of California and who himself had made his first fortune selling wholesale produce, opened the Bank of Italy in San Francisco in 1904. After the 1906 earthquake, Giannini supported the redevelopment of the city with assets kept secure in the bank's safes. He loaned money to working-class immigrants from ethnic communities throughout the state, ignoring the contemporary convention of localized banking. In 1928, he formed a holding company for his bank's many branches. This he called the Transamerica Corporation, and from this he formed Bank of America in 1930.

---

book of poetry with my name on its spine—would be published around my daughter's first birthday. The book tour was about honoring the years I'd spent writing in solitude. Years I'd spent creating an imaginative space all my own. I didn't want to slip into the kind of oblivion I visualized when I imagined women who stopped doing the things they'd previously done because they'd had a baby. I'd not yet been called to reassess my opinions about the changes motherhood demands of women. I wanted to remain the sort of woman who taught at a university, wrote books, and accepted invitations to speak about those books.

"Your generation is so different from ours," Mother repeated as I outlined my schedule while my father drove me to my job. She wanted to know how I intended to take care of the baby while I gallivanted around the country talking about my books. And what about my long hours at the office?

I sat in the backseat, my hand wrapped loosely around Callie's. Holding her like that made me relax. I couldn't store anger in my body, clench my fist, and risk hurting the baby. Relaxing was good. I didn't want to fight.

In the last trimester of my pregnancy I'd forgiven my mother. She hadn't actually done anything wrong. I wasn't forgiving the flesh-and-blood woman. I was pardoning the woman I'd constructed in my mind. I was pardoning "Mother," who questioned and cautioned and judged. As I contemplated what kind of mother I was likely to become, I realized that most of the time, when my mother asked questions and pushed against me and made me feel uncomfortable, she was voicing doubts I had also confronted. ▪

My mother was just a woman. She had opinions, but they needed be no more powerful or correct than any other woman's. Whatever fears or attitudes I attributed to her were no more hers than they were my own. I had made Mother the repository of my ideas about right and wrong. What I was irritated by was not Mother, not even her questions or the fears they conveyed, which felt unceasing, but the idea that someone would bring up questions I'd actively, and perhaps rashly, dismissed. Mother was a tedious bore, perpetually anxious about her first grandchild, but what she said to me, about me, was often true and always important.

I'd already done the worrying about how my travel companion would be received. At first I'd cautiously queried my hosts, but eventually I simply told people I was bringing my nursing daughter and we would need special accommodations. People

---

Safety

The Montgomery Block, the largest office building in the West at the time of its construction, was one of San Francisco's safest buildings in its day. Most structures erected in the mid–nineteenth century were made of wood, sometimes with oil-soaked canvas for walls and tarpaper for roofs. They were tinderboxes and frequently held stores of combustibles like ammunition and whiskey. But the Montgomery Block was brick. Not only did the building withstand the 1906 earthquake, it served as a fire block against the quake-incited fire that was, in fact, more culpable in destroying the city.

---

sounded tickled by the idea of helping me find a locally favored sitter for the hours I was scheduled to visit classes or deliver lectures. If not tickled, at least they weren't distressed. They promised to put me in hotels with refrigerators. They offered toys their grown children had left behind.

When she assured me she looked forward to meeting the baby during my upcoming visit to Pittsburgh, Toi Derricotte said the early days of motherhood were made less difficult for her by a community of helpful women. ∎

Saying this, she reminded me she'd been a mother and a writer

---

Community

When Joseph Strauss developed a daring design to bridge the channel between San Francisco and Marin, he could find no substantial financial backers. The Reconstruction Finance Corporation, established by Congress during Herbert Hoover's presidency, might have otherwise supported the project, but it had already overcommitted by promising more than $60 million toward the construction of the San Francisco–Oakland Bay Bridge. Convinced of the economic viability and necessity of a bridge connecting the city to the North Bay, in 1931 Giannini's Bank of America accepted the risk of bonds for the bridge's completion. This $6 million investment emboldened others; soon, Strauss had $35 million for constructing the Golden Gate Bridge. Though the San Francisco–Oakland Bay Bridge cost more, is longer, required greater feats of engineering, includes what was then the world's largest tunnel, accommodates the first and/or final miles of the transcontinental artery I-80, demanded one of the heaviest and longest cantilevers of all time, and was completed six months sooner, Strauss's bridge immediately and seemingly permanently became the more highly revered of the San Francisco Bay's spans.

---

as well. It's not something about which I should have needed reminding. The first book of hers I'd ever loved was called *Natural Birth*. But when I thought about who I was to become when I became a mother, I hadn't pictured Toi. I hadn't pictured anyone, really. When I thought about who I was to become when I became a mother, I mostly felt very alone.

I think of the period between learning I was pregnant and accepting my new life as a professional and a mother as a period when a fourth wall fell. At first I thought I was alone in a boxed-in space. I felt sure that the woman I'd worked thirty-six years to become would be pushed aside by someone else. I held off announcing the pregnancy, worried how my colleagues and mentors would take the news. But when I revealed my condition, I saw that I didn't have to disappear into oblivion. I would join a large community that had been there all along. People I'd known for years all of a sudden became parents. In my eyes, at least, it was all of a sudden. People who were the same people they'd been moments before, people I'd known and respected, revealed aspects of their lives I'd not had the privilege or inclination to see. Circumspect public figures told me intimate stories about their labor experiences. Women I knew as high-powered administrators glowed about their own pregnancies. Men I'd shared whiskey with for years manifested as fathers who were silly with their kids on Sunday mornings. Recounting all sorts of stories I'd not been able to hear before, people made it clear they were excited to welcome me into the company of parents.

"People seem to like the idea of having a baby around," I told Mother. "This will work. We will make this work." ▪

·

O N MONDAYS AND TUESDAYS, when I spent the day on my home campus, Ray would watch Callie during his less-productive morning hours. A friend who wanted to help Ray finish his dissertation and who wasn't averse to having a bit of extra cash would watch the baby in the afternoons and evenings. Thus, we'd resolved the child-care dilemma for the meantime.

"I think this is going to work," I told my parents once again. I wanted them to agree with me, but Dad said nothing. He was focused on keeping us safe on the traffic-saturated freeway. The population of California doubles every fifty years. For every person who gives up on the state, at least two are likely to take her place, joining their vehicles to the rest of ours.

Mother said, "It seems like you're trying to do too much."

"These readings are part of the life of a modern writer," I

Work

According to the *Los Angeles Times*, the unemployment rate in Alameda County, where we lived, was 11 percent in January 2011 when Callie was an infant. One of the paradoxes of California is that, though it is has been perceived as a land of opportunity since its fast-tracked introduction to statehood, the big booms that make the state so attractive mean that the busts hit more people in more severe ways. Waves of economic insolvency overlap with every major economic upswing the state has seen. In California, someone is always down on his luck.

---

reminded her. I felt I had to reaffirm this. I'd had a prolific phase as a writer and editor, and lest that work sink far below the radar, I needed to get out into the world and tell people what I'd been doing. I explained that these readings were equivalent to the talk show circuit required of actors when new movies are released. "Writers have to have a public face," I told her.

"I suppose so," Mother said, as she looked out the window at San Francisco's Financial District and its skyline. "I guess we just stopped working while we were raising our children, or we went half-time—"

"If you go to half-time," I interrupted, "you might as well stop working." I'd developed a bad habit of interrupting people around the time I went back to work. The minutes of my days were limited. I didn't have the luxury of waiting while someone formulated a conclusion I'd anticipated, particularly if the conclusion would reveal one of my own fears. "It's pretty hard to be a successful professional on a part-time basis," I continued. Though I interrupted others, I wanted to be sure I was fully heard myself.

"Yes. You're right, of course," sighed Mother.

Change and Renewal

What the great quake and fire of the early twentieth century could not destroy, urban renewal at the midcentury did. Just like the ships that brought the first flood of nineteenth century immigrants to the bay, the Montgomery Block, once home to Jack London, Mark Twain, Robert Louis Stevenson, Emma Goldman, Bret Harte, and Ambrose Bierce, is now but a memory under the footprint of the Transamerica building, the world's tallest pyramid.

Her own professional trajectory reflected this truth. Mother earned her master's degree when I was eighteen months old, but she didn't return for her Ph.D. until I went off to college. After I started the first grade, she cobbled together flexibly scheduled jobs, some related to her field of interest and some that simply allowed her to be home at a certain time to care for her children while her husband, a pediatrician, built his career. She is representative of so many. I can count seven women writers who told me that having a family cost them at least one book because of the ways they had to reorganize their lives to accommodate having children. "I have a son I love," said one prominent Bay Area writer, "and a rich life. But I'll never have that book. That book is gone forever."

Mother ended her professional career as an associate dean at a top-tier medical school. She was no slouch, certainly, and she managed all this while also serving on PTAs and providing snacks for my Girl Scout troop when it met at our house. Part of my drive comes from a desire to emulate my mother's success. Another part is fueled by my questions about what she might have achieved if she had begun her professional track before she was in her early fifties. ∎

The backseat of my parents' Lexus is designed to be more comfortable than it was on that particular drive. Already my breasts were filling, though I'd fed Callie just before we climbed into the car. It was hard going to the university to teach other people's children how to write when I would rather be home teaching my own daughter how to talk and walk and reason.

An hour or two into my time on campus I'd have to pump milk.

There was very little I hated more than pumping. The Medela Pump In Style I hauled around in its sleek black backpack stopped being low-profile the moment it was turned on. Then it sounded like heavy machinery. With the clear plastic cones— *flanges*—cupped over my breasts pulling meager amounts of milk up a tube and into a bottle, I felt like a nameless character in a science fiction movie where things end badly for the women.

After harvesting sufficient milk, I would stand in front of a lecture hall and talk about the historical context of a mid-twentieth century poem about a busload of people gawking at a moose and wonder if I'd remembered to insert a pad into my bra in case I started leaking.

Elizabeth Bishop, author of "The Moose," had no children. I don't know if this is important to her poetry. Anne Bradstreet, whose work I also teach, did have children, and they provided her with the experience she needed to write one of her most famous poems, "The Author to Her Book." But after Phillis Wheatley, the first black person to publish a book in English,

---

Accommodation

When the Transamerica building was first proposed, it was to be rectangular like other skyscrapers, but the tenants of buildings around the old Montgomery Block protested. They didn't want to be cut off from the Bay's legendary light. The tapered sides of the pyramid are an elegant accommodation, a way to allow the building to stand taller than any other, but with a slight shadow. I think about that sometimes as I construct myself as a mother. I want to be as big as I can be, but I aim to cast a lighter shadow on my daughter than some shadows I have known.

---

married and bore three babies, two of whom died in infancy, her days as a poet of record were done.

While I lectured on the precarious position of women poets in America, particularly black women poets, I worried that Callie would be crying because she disliked drinking from a bottle.

●

THE FIRST TIME I left her with my parents for the long Monday shift had not gone particularly well. I had given them plenty of diapers, toys, extra clothes and blankets, several bottles of pumped milk, pureed peas, and rice cereal. I had even given them some of the unopened formula samples that arrived in our mailbox within ten days of Callie's birth.

Formula companies buy birth records from hospitals or the county, and they use these to identify the addresses of new parents. When samples started arriving, I wondered what it must be like to suffer a stillbirth or a sudden infant death and receive formula, unbidden, in the mail. For such parents, the engine of capitalism must propel an unyeilding grief.

I tried not to feel guilty about leaving Callie because I understood as a matter of survival that, for working mothers, guilt is a waste of time. ■ Instead, I kept myself busy meeting with colleagues and teaching and pumping and meeting with students about their course of study and grading and pumping and teaching and advising graduate students on the poems that they found time, amid their own hectic schedules, to write.

When I'd finally driven across the Bay Bridge after that first day back to work, I kept busy listening to some of the *Freakonomics* podcasts I didn't get to listen to when a baby who wanted soothing music was strapped into a car seat in the back of my little red car. Focused on driving on a busy freeway at night and listening to Stephen Dubner talk about grown-up ideas, I could stop fretting over the things that typically jumbled through my mind.

I wasn't distracted by thinking about whether or not Callie was breathing, whether or not Ray would get a job, whether or not I would lose my belly fat, how much work I had ahead of me, whether or not Callie was sleeping, whether or not I would get any sleep that night myself. My thoughts did not leap from one worry to another, from one preoccupation to the next, from one line of inquiry to another, as they so often tend to do. My attention was focused on thinking about how amazing it was that the Chinese taste for chicken feet meant Perdue Farms could ship billions of chicken feet across the ocean, thus preventing an enormous amount of animal by-product from entering the U.S. waste stream. I actually felt good when I walked through the

---

Projection

At 853 feet, the Transamerica Pyramid is the tallest building in Northern California. When it was completed in 1972 (the year I was born), it was the tallest building west of the Mississippi River, designed to be a grand representation of a bold and influential world city. The scuttled ships and crisscrossed logs that stretched the city for blocks beyond the natural waterline were exposed again as the building's base was established. The pyramid would look taller if it weren't built on some of the city's most sunken ground.

---

door of my parents' vacation condo. I felt a bit like my old self would feel if my old self had engorged breasts.

"You didn't leave us with enough milk," Mother snapped the moment I walked in. ∎

This was not what I wanted to hear upon seeing my daughter for the first time in more than twelve hours.

"She didn't want her food, and she drank through all her milk almost immediately," Mother said.

"What about the milk I put in the freezer?"

"She drank it all."

"I thought I'd left enough." I tried to say this calmly. "She's never gone through that much milk before. Did you try the formula?"

"She wouldn't touch the formula," Mother scolded, "and refused cereal. You'll need to bring more milk. She was hungry all day. Couldn't be consoled."

I took the baby from her grandmother's arms and sat in a quiet place to calm her.

I was trying to be a good mother.

Treasure

In the first months of 1848, James Marshall found gold flakes while building a sawmill on John Sutter's land along the American River. Within two years, the California Territory became a state, as the population grew by more than a hundred thousand fortune-seekers. It was in response to this rush that the elder Peralta reminded his sons that the source of their wealth was their land, warning them away from fickle gold mines.

I let Callie nurse for longer than usual. Eventually, she stopped crying. She'd suckled to her heart's content. ∎

Once she settled down, I reached into the travel cooler I'd lugged to campus and extracted the six ounces I'd pumped. This little bit I'd leave for the next day. We'd augment the short supply with stock I kept in our apartment's freezer.

When I first started pumping, I was alarmed. I had pumped for thirty minutes as instructed. How could I possibly feed my baby with just the little bit of milk that swirled at the bottom of the bottle?

I called a friend who had pumped and nursed her sons to their second birthdays.

"I don't have enough milk!" I cried into the phone.

"It comes slowly sometimes," she assured me.

"But in the videos—"

"Ugh, those videos," she interrupted. "You were expecting to be like a cow or something, right? Just shooting milk into a pail?"

Boundaries

For the Peraltas, mapping meant describing a boundary in relationship to particular landmarks. They would indicate how many acres lay between the two tallest redwood trees in the foothills and their hacienda in the fertile valley, triangulating those references against the estuarial lake, now call Lake Merritt, formed by creeks in their rush toward the bay. The creeks and their courses were mapped, too. Highlands and valleys, fertile land and natural irrigation, existing labor sources and a long growing season: the Peraltas' land held endless potential.

"I think so, yes."

She took a deep breath. "It's not like that for most of us." ■

"Milk can come slowly," she continued, "but you'll make enough, don't worry. Remember, babies' bellies are small. They don't need as much as you or I would need." She paused briefly. "And don't listen when they say you need to throw away the bottle if the baby hasn't finished the whole thing. You put that bottle right back into the refrigerator." A deep exhalation, and she was finished on the subject.

When I went back to work the next day, I knew that my parents would have to give Callie whatever fresh and frozen milk I had. I knew this possibly would not be enough. I'd have to build up a much larger store.

I sat in my parents' vacation condo after my first long day of work and thought, I can't keep my baby fed. ■

Thirty minutes later, as I was packing our gear for the drive

---

Abundance

During the gold rush, many of the wealthiest new Californians made their money by selling goods to the miners, not in mining for precious metal themselves. Think of the Hills Brothers selling canned coffee. Levi Strauss selling sturdy denim trousers. Think of Mr. Studebaker, who made his first fortune selling wheelbarrows to prospectors. Think of Henry Wells and William Fargo, who had the foresight to set up banking operations in San Francisco. Then there were the Americanos who made their fortunes selling land. Land like the Peralta land. Land like John Sutter's. Think of the Rancho San Antonio's first squatter, Moses Chase. Chase is known now as the founder of the town of Clinton, which would eventually become part of Oakland but was originally a plot of usurped Peralta land.

---

home, Callie cried for milk again. I put everything down and prepared to nurse.

"That's why you don't have enough milk," Mother scolded. "You're always feeding her."

The truth of Mother's contradictory accusation was not lost on me.

One of the discomforts of parenthood is that people can come at you with several contradictory statements, and you must acknowledge the truth in the lot. Callie had been fussy all day because she was accustomed to being nursed on demand and, because when I was with her I allowed her to nurse on demand, I didn't have much milk when I tried to pump. She didn't love the bottle and was skeptical of solid food, and for the first months of her life I was on hand most anytime she required me. When I went back to work, I developed a complicated system that allowed me to be with her as much as possible, so there was still no need for her to grow accustomed to the bottle or alternative foods. She hadn't ever had to go without fresh milk very long. But now that my life had returned to the sort of schedule I wanted and needed, and that I wanted to

---

Empty

John Sutter's property was trashed by the onslaught of gold seekers. Deeply in debt, he handed over the deed to his son, who had big plans. The transaction brought Sutter no great wealth. He returned to Pennsylvania a bitter man, frustrated that the city built on his former property was known as Sacramento, not something more like Suttersville.

---

believe would be the best for my daughter, Callie and I both had to adjust. That would not be easy. ▪

•

TWICE ALREADY, I'd driven short distances for campus speaking engagements and left Callie with her grandparents. On both occasions, women in the departments I visited lent me their offices, where I set up my Medela Pump In Style, which loudly whirred and sucked away.

On the first such trip, my host, a woman I knew from my single days, sat in the office with me and gossiped about people we knew in common. After my pumping session during the next visit, the professor in the adjacent office came into the hall to tell me she remembered how, during her own pumping days, the woman who occupied the office in which I'd pumped used to

---

Ownership

The courts recognized the deed that Sutter gave his son. Not so for the Peraltas. Squatters destroyed and usurped and leased and then sold and deforested and developed the Peralta land. The Peralta brothers took their case to the Lands Commission and had their first verdict in 1854, but they appeared again in the U.S. District Court in 1855. The case for their land went to the U.S. Supreme Court in 1857. It wasn't until 1877 that Peralta heirs received a patent for their land from the U.S. government. Two years later, the last son died in a house on land the Spanish had once granted his family. His people called the place Rancho San Antonio, but now folks call the area Fruitvale because a settler from Iowa planted his orchards there.

---

knock on the wall and yell, "Moo. Moo." This was meant to make me feel better about pumping milk for a child I'd left behind. This was meant to remind me I was a woman, not just a mom. This was meant to remind me I wasn't alone.

"You have a nice time with your granddaughter today," I told my parents as their Lexus approached the campus. I was tired already from the difficult commute, and the workday had not yet begun.

Much of what I had thought would make me tired had become par for the course by the time the new semester started. Callie had been sleeping more successfully through the night since her sixth-month birthday. Rather than take this gift of time to get some rest myself, in order to build a stockpile of milk I had been staying up to pump in the half hour at midnight when the baby used to wake for a feeding. These were hours of sleep I'd not experienced for months, and so they did not seem to have been stolen from me. Their loss had already been accounted for.

I was the kind of pregnant woman who read book after book as I tried to understand what was happening to my body and the body of the baby inside me. When I read books about pregnancy I learned not to read more than two months ahead. If I started reading the labor and delivery chapter in my first trimester, everything sounded terrifying, unreal, and impossible. Once I was thirty-four weeks pregnant, and the ligaments in my pelvis loosened alarmingly to allow room for a person who would only continue to grow, it was a relief to read two chapters ahead and learn that I'd have to go through a bit of pain and gore but at the end of this process (which I read about, then, with keen interest)

I'd have a person and, with proper exercise and lots of nursing, I'd get some approximation of my old body back.

In the first weeks after Callie was born, I'd wake in the middle of the night drenched in sweat. I slept on a towel, my body had so much excess water to shed. This was normal. Case histories in the pregnancy and parenthood books warned me about hormonal fluctuations that caused night sweats.

What I hadn't accounted for were my night terrors. ▪

The books warned me that the flood of hormones related to pregnancy and birth, coupled with the sleep deprivation and emotional sensitivity triggered by caring for a helpless person, might make me particularly sensitive. But, as every woman's emotional sensitivity is unique, unlike the relative similarity of the final stages of a baby's route out of a woman's body, there could be no textbook illustrations.

The books could prepare me for the fact that I would react to the world differently than I might have reacted before, but only experience would teach me the ways these differences would manifest.

It was this generally experienced and yet incredibly personal psychological discomfort that kept me up at night.

Unknown Territory

The mode of mapping used by Californios like the Peraltas was as foreign to the newly arrived Americanos as their language. What good does a map of landmarks do if those landmarks are irrevocably changed? Cut down trees and blast a boulder, reroute a creek with sludge from mining runoff, and tear down a house. Now there are no landmarks left to prove a claim.

There was so much at stake now that the fourth wall had fallen.

I was connected to more people—had a bigger family. I was exposed to a much larger network of success and failure.

I worried about the safety of those I loved. I worried about tsunamis, debt, car accidents, brown recluse spiders, who would care for my baby, and how we were going to survive. I worried about the 20 percent of children in Alameda County—our home—who experienced food insecurity in 2011. I saw these children around me all the time. I knew some of their names. If I could put a face to suffering, I would call that suffering face into my dreams. ▪

•

MY FATHER IDLED beside the Humanities Building, where I would spend another workday. Bordered by native plants and accessible pathways, the five-story building rose above the campus surrounding it. I kissed Callie's forhead, trying to cen-

---

Rediscovery

In the late twentieth century, a woman saw a picture of the subdivided house where she'd grown up and also a picture of the Peralta Hacienda and she realized they were one and the same. She spearheaded a renovation project, and now the Peralta Hacienda is a historic site. I passed the sign for the landmark every time I took the Fruitvale Avenue exit off I-580 on my way home, but I had no idea what it referred to until one day, when Callie still cried constantly unless she was moving, I strapped her into the stroller and walked until I found the place, which is how I started to know some of the things I've written here.

---

ter myself in the pleasure of our last moments together, but her attention was drawn by my office building's glinting windows.

"Goodbye," I told my family, "and good luck."

As they pulled away, I remembered ascending the escalator at the Montgomery BART station during a trip into San Francisco. This was Tuesday, October 26, 2010. Callie was nearly five months old. Her whole body arched toward the long reach of sky. She was harnessed to me as I bore her along, her six-inch trunk secured between my breasts. She was arching away from my body so she could follow the trajectory of the skyscrapers all the way to the place where their antennae tried to scrape the Northern California sun. We were on the way to City Lights Bookstore where I was due to give a poetry reading, but she didn't care about that. She wedged her arms and legs against my belly for support as she bent back, back, and farther back, mouth open in what looked like hunger. I'd been wearing her this close to my body all her life, and I'd never felt her exert a will like this before. I hadn't felt her work so hard to push away from me.

Callie was looking at the tallest buildings she had ever seen, and she needed her whole self for this looking.

LAP CHILD

⸺

f I keep the baby with me when I go to the bathroom, I have
to struggle into the airplane lavatory, nudging my upper body
over the commode far enough so I can turn around and lock the
door, ignoring the crazed fear that the BabyBjörn securing Callie
to my stomach might fail and force me to watch her slide past the
flap at the bottom of the toilet. If I manage to turn the front of
my body back toward the door without knocking the baby's head
against the lavatory walls or running her feet through the sink
area's standing pools of water, I have to balance myself over the
commode despite my altered center of gravity. I push the Baby-
Björn up and away from my belly to undo my pants, and then
lower myself over the toilet. All the while, turbulence works to
unsteady me. There is the awkward negotiation of toilet paper to
contend with. Then I have to squat, jutting my tailbone out and
dropping my chest, thus allowing the BabyBjörn-bound baby to
fall away from my torso so I can pull my pants back up. Buttons
always prove my final foil. More than once I have walked out of

the lavatory unbuttoned, returning to my seat before I can take Callie out of the BabyBjörn and finally fasten my pants. Like so much of motherhood, going to the bathroom while wearing a baby demands equal parts acrobatic prowess, fear management, and sublimation of shame. So, when a grandmother returning from Florida said, "I'll be happy to help you," and meant, *I would love to hold your baby,* as we boarded our flight from Logan to the Northern Maine Regional Airport, I said she could hold her as soon as we took off, hoping I could pee in peace.

As it turned out, using the bathroom, with or without the baby, was not an option on this flight. The moment the propellers began their one-and-a-half-hour sound show, Callie resorted to the infant's best defense against chaos: deep slumber a mother dares not disturb.

We were in our final descent when the man sitting next to me leaned closer so I could hear him over the noise of the propellers. "I have to admit," he admitted, "I was worried when you two sat down. Babies, you know." He placed his earplugs in a carrying case he then placed in his backpack. "I commute every couple weeks. Three weeks on, two weeks off. Been doing that since I took a job with Exxon eighteen months ago." Jobs were, he told me, scarce in the part of Aroostook County he called home, and though the travel could be hard, the pay was good and the work steady. "I don't usually like flying with babies," he said. "These planes are loud enough as it is." I nodded. I don't usually like flying with babies, either. "But she's a good one, isn't she?" Yes, I said. She was. And then he told me about his girlfriend and how he wondered what their house would look like when he got back, seeing as the dog he'd bought her for Christmas took advantage when he was away. "You know how it is," he said, because the baby provided him with a way to connect with me.

It was nine-thirty p.m. and nineteen degrees when we landed in the northeasternmost county of the contiguous United States. Before heading out across the tarmac, I wrapped Callie's blanket over the BabyBjörn, and around this bundle I pulled the over-sized parka my husband lends me when I visit cold places. The oil rig worker carried Callie's diaper bag down the airstairs. A businessman carried our backpack. I didn't ask for any of this. Everyone just seemed to understand what needed to be done.

In baggage claim, I gave the baby to the woman whose grand-children were in Florida so I could haul our luggage off the car-ousel. Immediately she plowed her nose into Callie's hair. "If I could bottle that smell," she said, because babies are simultane-ously astounding and mundane and so are the things people do around them.

When I returned for the baby, she took one last deep breath, smiled as if she was genuinely glad for the opportunity to fly on a prop plane with us, gathered her own bags, and disappeared.

"This is the baby I was telling you about," a man told his wife as he moved to fill the departed grandmother's space. I'd noticed this man watching us in the waiting area at Logan. We'd smiled the smile of acknowledgment passed between black people countrywide, but he hadn't approached us until now, with his innocuous-looking wife by his side. I was putting Callie back in the BabyBjörn to free my hands to move our luggage toward the cabstand. This process stalled as the man told me he lived nearby in Caribou, described Caribou (the second-largest city in the least populous county of the state), and shrugged off my query about the cold. "I've been in Maine such a long time I hardly notice the climate anymore," he said, looking around the room to make sure I understood.

In the same way that we both understood our silent greeting in Logan meant, *It's nice to see another black person*, he figured I understood what he meant about the climate. He was a black man, a big one at that, living in cold, white, northern Maine. I gathered people often eyed him with suspicion. People use foils to help them express their desires. They use excuses. They try to hold their tongues. They speak poetically, working through connotation and association. "I'd be happy to help while you carry your luggage to the cab," he said. He wasn't offering to help me haul the luggage. What he wanted was to hold the baby. Perhaps had wanted to do so since he first laid eyes on us, but to openly admit a desire to hold a stranger's child can be risky.

The woman who held Callie while I got my luggage off the carousel had taken a long time to articulate her desire as well. At Logan, she positioned herself across from us in the waiting area. "Your daughter looks like a little angel," she said. "I just left my three grandchildren in Florida," she said. Then she pulled back into herself. It hadn't occurred to me that she wanted to hold the baby. It is possible it hadn't occurred to her, either. Part of the joy of watching the baby was watching her move.

Callie had been successfully crawling for less than a month, so she moved through space with the confidence of a master and the coordination of a novice. In January, she started crawling backward, not forward, which seemed to frustrate her. Then she began to skooch herself forward in such a way that I found myself comparing my darling girl to some sort of animal: a lizard with a low center of gravity and four unstrategically splayed limbs. She'd get a leg stuck on the wrong side of an arm, her little butt would shake, and down she'd go, forced to figure out how to roll off her side, sit back up, and try again. This was what we called progress in our house for several weeks. But during the last week of February, around the time her first tooth erupted, Callie began to propel herself forward in earnest.

First step, crawling, we said. Next step, the world!

It was the middle of March when Callie and I flew to Maine. On the plane from San Francisco to Boston, Callie kept her voice and body perfectly contained in our seat. She even chose her naptime to coincide with the entire in-flight movie, which happened to be the year's Oscar-winning film *The King's Speech*. A movie I had not yet had a chance to see. As we walked off the plane, people remarked on how quiet she had been, how they didn't even realize there'd been a baby on board. There are things over which I have little control, and yet they fill me with a nearly sinful degree of pride. My baby's immense public composure is one of these.

In Logan, when she had space to move, I wanted to reward her with the freedom to move. I let her crawl on the parka's cozy interior lining, picking her up only as long as it took to keep her off the dirty airport floor. The grandmother across from us watched. The man I later learned lived in Caribou watched. I watched. The woman sitting next to me watched. Callie crawled. I repositioned her on the parka. Callie crawled some more.

"This is my first time back to Maine in over twenty years," the woman sitting next to me said to the air someplace in front of Callie. When I asked what had kept her away so long, she told Callie the story. "My father hadn't wanted me to go to college, but I went anyway. That was what women were doing, and I wanted to be a woman. I was a woman," she said.

Callie was crawling toward the edge of the parka. I moved her back toward the center and she crawled toward the edge of the parka again. I was listening to the woman mostly as a way to pass time.

"That was the start of it, anyway. After I graduated, I moved to the city." A gate agent came over the intercom, and the woman waited to determine whether the message would be of any consequence to us. It was not. "One day my parents came for a visit. They hadn't told me they were coming. I was living with my boyfriend to save money. And because I loved him, of course. I did love him." I overheard the woman, but I was no more relevant than a priest in a confessional is relevant to a person unburdening herself before a silent God. "Well, anyway, my father never spoke to me again."

The woman watched Callie rattle a tub of chocolate-covered raisins and work the plastic toward her mouth. I didn't have a chance to say anything. I just grabbed the tub of chocolate-covered raisins out of Callie's hands.

The raisins came from Au Bon Pain, where I'd stopped for a

sandwich on my way to our gate. The woman working the counter hardly talked to me. She was focused on the baby. Her little feet. Her little hands. Her little smile. Her little feet. Her little hands. Her little smile. I stood with the baby's back BabyBjörned to my belly, waiting until the cashier stopped playing with my daughter's little feet long enough to take my order.

My birthday is just before New Year's Eve, so, rather than making a New Year's resolution, I articulate birthday intentions. I think of something I want to work on in my character and try to work on it throughout the new year. One year I worked on learning how to turn down offers from men that sound too good to be true. One year I tried to stop worrying about things over which I had no control. Sometimes I have to remediate. For years thirty-three through thirty-five I worked on patience. I had to be patient with myself as I tried to learn patience, but now that I had a baby I couldn't help but be patient. I have earned my Ph.D. in patience. Call me Professor Patience, please. The Au Bon Pain cashier played with Callie's little fingers, her little faux-shoes. She looked up long enough to take my order and plug it into the register, then she went right back to tickling Callie's little calf.

I don't mind all the time it takes to weave through other people's responses to my daughter because it gives me space to live in my own head. I took my time putting the change from my sandwich back into my wallet, thinking about the house I wanted so badly and which seemed an impossible dream. When I looked up, I realized Callie had a tub of $6 chocolate-covered raisins in her hands. I didn't know if she'd picked the carton up or if the woman behind the counter had given them to her, but when I tried to pay for the raisins, the cashier shook her head and waved her hand. She didn't look at me. Instead, she poked her finger toward the baby's belly, steadily holding my daughter's gaze. "For you," she said, as if, if she could, she would give my child the whole world.

In the waiting room for the flight to Maine, the woman sitting next to me watched as I took the raisins out of Callie's hands and put them in my backpack because Callie watched me put the raisins in the backpack. When Callie crawled toward the far end of the parka, she watched me pick her up and move her back to the middle. When Callie turned her attention toward her own toes, the woman said to Callie's toes, "Your mother loves you, and you know it." Callie pulled her toes closer to her mouth.

"My mother used to visit me in Boston every once in a while," the woman said, "but my father never came." She stared at Callie the way I focus on the kitten posters in the phlebotomist's office, so I can keep my mind on something good. "It's been about fifteen years since I talked to either of them. He has dementia real bad now," she said. "I'm going back to help my mother. She can't take care of him alone." Callie crawled toward us, and I picked her up just as the gate agent called our flight. I had started the process of consolidating our carry-ons when the woman said, "Let me hold her for you," and I placed my baby in her waiting arms.

"Oh!" said the grandmother whose children were in Florida. She sighed as if she'd just realized there was a contest she could have won if only she'd entered on time.

THIS WAS THE LONGEST TRIP Callie and I had taken together, the first time since she was born that I had traveled to a speaking engagement hosted by a stranger. The invitation to visit the University of Maine, Fort Kent, where we were headed the next day, came only a week after I spoke on air with Renee Montagne about the anthology of African American nature poetry I'd edited, the first collection of its kind. The campus and surrounding community would host classes, round-table discussions, and a writing contest related to my book. The work I'd done in private was being spoken about in cars and kitchens and planning rooms that I'd never known to imagine before.

Though I consider poetry a mode of communication, it has always felt intimate to me. "I write as if I am whispering in the ear of the one I love," says Terry Tempest Williams in her essay "Why I Write." I use poetry to understand myself, to understand the people who are near to me. I live a writer's life and hope to change the world one person at a time. I write in the dark, groping and unsure, but heeding instincts I've been learning to guide. Something in me needs to believe no one is looking, so I can take the risks I need to take to make the writing come out right. I assumed the way I'd conducted my writing life was how it would always be. But after that interview on NPR, I was born into another life. My private artistic life became public at the same time my domestic life began to reveal itself to the world. My belly had just started to swell when I received the invitation from UMFK. I was growing and changing before the public eye.

"Our first baby is due this June, and I'd not planned on doing any events next spring," I wrote Professor Jenny Radsma, "but I have to admit that your invitation is too tempting to turn down. The caveat for me is that, as I will still be nursing, I will likely bring my baby along." This was one of the strangest business emails I had ever written. When I hit send, I felt as if I'd put my belly and breasts on display when no one had asked to see either.

"What an exciting time for you, to welcome your firstborn!" Dr. Radsma responded, unfazed. She told me the best way to travel to Fort Kent: The baby and I would take a day-long flight from San Francisco to Boston, then a small plane to Presque Isle, and the next day, when the sun was up and we were rested, someone would drive us the remaining ninety minutes to Fort Kent. Everything was possible. Babies happen to people every day, Dr. Radsma's email suggested. Folks would accommodate mine.

And so I prepared for a winter trip to Maine.

The suitcase I packed was filled with tiny snowsuits, sweaters, and cozy sweatpants mailed to us by friends and family from Iowa, Michigan, and Vermont. The baby clothes were accompanied by advice on how to keep a hat on a reluctant baby's head, how to keep mittens on a reluctant baby's hands, and how to keep a baby warm in a car seat. (Put bulky insulation over the straps or risk interfering with the protective powers of the five-point harness should you hit a moose.) I brought along the notes. I packed three outfits Callie could wear on each of our four days away, sixteen total if you counted alternate pairings, because I wanted to layer, and because I didn't know how casual or dressy northern Maine would be, because there could be spit-up or blow-outs, but mostly because I didn't want to leave cute cold-weather clothes in a drawer in California when they could serve a genuine purpose in northern Maine.

In case her feet got into something wet or dirty, I brought all three pairs of Callie's shoes, which were really just socks that snapped around her ankles. I also packed a pair of baby Uggs my mother had not been able to resist buying for her only grandchild. I packed tights whose feet looked like Mary Janes and tights whose legs were covered in flowers. I packed baby leg warmers, and when I realized I didn't have a suitable scarf for a nine-month-old, I wrote Jenny Radsma and asked if she could scare one up. I packed three pairs of her pajamas because I didn't know where we would find a washing machine. I packed two blankets, a sleep sack, burp clothes, a bath towel, and two washcloths. Hotel towels are so harsh I worried they'd rub Callie's new skin raw. On later trips, I'd pack a rubber duck or a bath toy to make an unfamiliar bath seem more familiar, but I had not yet thought of that.

In a Ziploc bag, I packed extra bottles, a bowl, and a couple of little spoons. I packed several jars of baby food. Certainly they must have grocery stores in northern Maine, but I didn't know if I'd have time to shop. I brought two packages each of the compostable wipes and diapers that made me feel slightly less horrible about all the waste we discarded. I packed three large compostable bags to hold this waste. I brought $5 bills to leave for the hotel cleaning crew.

I packed a black baby doll named Naima because when I left Callie with sitters during my presentations, I wanted her to have a familiar face nearby. I packed an Angel Dear mini-blanket given to me by the poet Rigoberto González at a board meeting we'd both attended in Portland, Maine, while I was nineteen weeks pregnant and recovering from a broken leg. I had been worried about that trip, too, but it had turned out well. The Angel Dear mini-blanket was supposed to be for Callie, but I probably packed it for me.

I packed a stuffed blue dinosaur that played "You Are My Sunshine" when Callie squeezed it. I packed *Olivia* and *Hug*. I packed *The Snowy Day* and the nonmaterialistic version of *Hush, Little Baby*, because they talked about mother love and snow day fun. I packed baby shampoo, hair detangler, barrettes, her comb, her brush, rubber bands. I packed baby lotion, diaper cream. I packed nasal saline spray and a nasal aspirator in case she got congested from the flight.

I put my things in one corner of the suitcase: one pair of black pants, three tops, two dresses, tights, socks, underwear, nursing pads, and an extra set of glasses because I did not want to be thirty-three hundred miles from home when Callie broke my only pair.

In the Northern Maine Regional Airport at Presque Isle, I slung the Pack 'n Play over my shoulder while I balanced the diaper bag and backpack in the car seat that was locked into the stroller, then I pushed the stroller/luggage cart with one hand and pulled our steamer-trunk-sized suitcase with the other. With everything thus precariously balanced, I left Callie in the arms of the black man from Caribou, and I headed toward the cabstand with our things.

The cabdriver had just finished loading another fare when I arrived. "You have everything but the kitchen sink," he said.

A wintry wind whipped around us. I tried to make sure my face was positioned in a manner that would discourage further small talk.

"I'm running the pilot and the flight attendant to their hotel. Mind if I come back for you?" What choice did I have? How many cabs could be running this late in Presque Isle? My particular response was no more important to him than it had been to anyone I'd talked to that day. "Just leave your things there," the driver said. "I'll load you up when I get back."

With the backpack and the diaper bag, I hurried out of the cold to reclaim my daughter, who was grinning to a song being sung by the wife of the man from Caribou.

"Folks must really trust each other here," I said, indicating the pile I'd left unattended in front of the airport terminal. No armed guards patrolled the building watching for potential security risks.

"Who would want to steal your things?" the woman asked, handing Callie back to me.

•

I SAT IN THE WAITING AREA, chatting with the solitary ticket agent while I nursed Callie. Then we watched Callie pull herself into a standing position with the aid of one of the airport's ten chairs. The baby sat down. I stood up and paced. By now it was nearly ten p.m. We were the only travelers remaining. The baby pulled herself up. I sat down and talked to the ticket agent again. She had been marshaler, ramp agent, and baggage thrower, too. She could do a final security check and go home once we left. "It shouldn't be much longer," she said. "Twenty minutes or so." With Callie in the BabyBjörn, I headed toward the bathroom. "I'd be happy to hold her while you're in there," the ticket agent said. She would be a Callie minder, too.

It was possible I stayed in the bathroom longer than was necessary so I could enjoy the quiet feeling of being behind a locked door attending to only myself for the first time since five-thirty A.M.

Before the worry kicked in and I raced to wash up, only to find Callie flexing her leg muscles on the ticket counter, the sole remaining airport employee's hands steady on her waist; before the only cab in Presque Isle returned to collect us; before I secured the car seat in the back of the cab while the driver loaded the suitcase and the stroller and the Pack 'n Play and the backpack and the diaper bag in the trunk, saying, "You brought everything but the kitchen sink"; before the driver started driving us through dark streets, toward some snowy town; before he told me how he used to drive trucks and his wife would pack "for four days if I was gone four weeks, for four weeks if I was gone four days—'Woman, what is wrong with you?' I'd say, 'I'm gone for four days and you pack for a month. I'm gone for a month and you pack for four days'"; before I realized he was so accustomed to running over the same road again and again and again that his speech patterns had to circle back, too; before, without my giving him an address or the proper hotel name, we pulled up to the Presque Isle Inn & Convention Center, which looked a lot like a two-story motel; before he helped me haul the luggage into the lobby, shaking his head and saying, "You packed everything but the kitchen sink"; before I checked in and made two trips from the lobby to our room with the luggage and one trip to the vending machine; before I set up the Pack 'n Play; before I took a chip bag out of Callie's hands and prompted the day's first steady stream of tears; before I quelled her tears with the stuffed blue dinosaur; before I set her in the Pack 'n Play; before she had her first poop of the day and cried and cried and cried and cried and cried until I changed her diaper and took her, clean, into my arms, reciting Blake's "Jerusalem" and "The Idea of Order at Key West" by Wallace Stevens; before she let her limbs relax and fell asleep; I stood, several moments longer than necessary, in the accessible stall of the Northern Maine Regional Airport's two-stall bathroom, alone.

When I pray for traveling mercies, I am praying for moments like these.

A SHADE NORTH OF ORDINARY

On our first and only morning in Presque Isle, Maine, Callie and I ventured to the Presque Isle Inn & Convention Center's breakfast lounge. I ate the complimentary breakfast. Callie ate rice cereal mixed with the pureed peas and Asian pear I'd brought from California. The breakfast lounge attendant asked me how we were, what we were doing in Presque Isle. I told her I was passing through on the way to give a presentation at the university in Fort Kent. The breakfast lounge attendant asked how we were finding the visit so far, and I told her I knew about Presque Isle because of my interest in Maine's history and looked forward to exploring the town once we had eaten. The breakfast lounge attendant asked if we found our room okay, what we thought of the snow, what we thought of the cold, and I answered all of her questions. The special attention meant the baby and I didn't have to eat alone.

As we left the restaurant, the desk clerk asked how we were enjoying our stay so far, if we'd been able to adjust the thermostat to our satisfaction, if we'd enjoyed our breakfast, if we would be staying in Maine for long. It seemed this hotel specialized in personal attention. Closer to our room, both of the hotel maids we encountered in the hall stopped folding towels so they could ask me if my room was all right, how long I'd be in Presque Isle, how I was liking Maine so far, if I was bothered by the snow. "Isn't that baby precious," said the blonder of the two housekeepers. "Would you just look at all her hair!"

This degree of inquisitivness, directed at me, reminded me of a trip I once took to Achill Island, off the west coast of Ireland. I'd gone to visit friends who were living for the summer in the Heinrich Böll Cottage, a space that had been converted after Böll's death from the writer's family residence to a visiting artists' studio space. My friends, the Irish and American artists Helen O'Leary and Paul Chidester, both had major shows they were preparing, and they wanted to make the most of their time in the cottage. While Helen and Paul worked into the early afternoon, I'd stroll to the pub to drop letters in the postbox. This round-trip journey would have taken Helen or Paul twenty minutes, but it never failed to be a full morning's adventure for me.

All along the path, island residents emerged from their whitewashed raised gable houses. "How are you today?" they'd ask. "Staying up at the Böll house, are you?" they'd ask. "How are you finding it on Achill?" they'd ask. "You're only visiting us five days, are you? Can't stay longer?" they'd ask. What are they feeding you? Have you tried the black sausage? Have you tried the soda bread? How do you find the black sausage? How do you find the soda bread? Heading down to the pub? Fancy a bit of Guinness? Have some postcards to send, do you? Want to tell your family about Achill? The wind gets so bad here some winters it could carry away a young child. Did you know that? Fancy a bit of Harp, do you? All down the lane and back again this continued.

Toward the end of my stay, Paul took me to a family home for dinner. As the meal was prepared, my hosts set me up at the table, a Harp lager in hand and some cheddar cheese and soda bread on a cutting block nearby. The resident children and their friends, ages four, six, seven, seven, and nine, crawled and climbed and wove themselves around my chair, peppering me with questions.

This was 1998, and visitors were still rare in that part of Ireland. The children were friendly and inquisitive. They wanted to know all about America. What was New York City like? They found it hard to imagine I'd never been, that New York was as far from my home in California as it was from their home on Achill. What was California like? Did I know any movie stars? Had I ever been to an NBA game? What was an NBA game like? Did I know any rappers? Was I wearing makeup?

I do not, as a rule, wear makeup, so this final question, raised by the four-year-old, threw me for a moment. Then I put his question in context with the other questions. Just as these kids had never met a person from California, they had never seen a real live black person. They'd only seen black people on TV. Either I was wearing makeup that made me black, or I was something equally unreal, a rapper or someone who personally knew movie stars.

In fact, I did know several screen actors. I'd grown up in a community where such acquaintances were not unusual. But I didn't complicate our conversation with this information. The actors I knew were mostly just people like you and like me. They were not extraordinary in the ways my inquisitors imagined them to be.

"No, I'm not wearing makeup," I told the kid. "This is the color of my skin." He was too young to hide his disbelief. "We all have different-colored skin," I assured him. "Your sister's eyes are blue, aren't they?" The boy and his sister both nodded. "And yours are brown, and your friend's eyes are green."

"My mother's eyes are gray," said one of the seven-year-olds.

"Those are pretty rare in some parts of the world, gray eyes," I said. "But some people have gray eyes, and it's normal for them. It's the same with skin. Some of you have freckles, some of you don't." The youngest boy looked at his arm as if he were noticing his own freckles for the first time. "I have brown skin. That's the way I've always been. It doesn't come off." He reached for my arm to verify my assertion. Soon all the children were rubbing my arm, and it wasn't long before they were also playing with my hair, which was braided into the pencil-width, shoulder-length braids that were popular among African American women in the latter part of the twentieth century. The children touched my extensions and asked how long it took to braid my hair, if I washed it, how often I washed it, how I washed it, what my hair would look like if I let out the braids.

The adults had turned from their kitchen tasks. Two of them sat down at the table and pretended to be interested in the ched-

dar. They looked sheepish at first, listening in a falsely noncha-
lant manner, but soon enough the four-year-old's mother asked,
"How long does it take you to undo all those braids?" and I found
myself giving the whole household a lesson about the care and
styling of black hair.

It occurred to me, then, that the adults who slowed my progress from the Böll Cottage to the postbox had been asking me
questions about wind and black sausage instead of what they
really wanted to know. What they really wanted to know was
whether a black person like me was put off by Western Ireland's
brutal weather. They wanted to know about my hair, which
seemed so different from their own. They wanted to discuss the
ways I was different from them without having to say the word
black. They wanted to know who I was, and what I was doing on
their island, and how long I would stay, and if I would bring other
people like me. They did not want to know all these things out of
malice. They were simply curious, and they were looking for the
most polite ways to express their curiosity. I didn't look like the
ordinary visitor, after all. And so it was, as I moved through the
Presque Isle Inn & Convention Center at a reduced speed due to
all the questions I was fielding, that part of me wondered what
the breakfast host, and desk clerk, and housekeepers wanted to
know besides what I thought of the weather.

I stopped long enough to let the housekeepers get a good look
at the baby. Callie does have marvelous hair. The morning she
was born, her hair was so thick the OB needed three attempts
to successfully secure the cranial monitor he used to track her
progress through the birth canal. When she finally emerged,

Callie's eyes were wide open and she didn't cry. They cut the cord, and she didn't cry. The nurses washed her body. They showed Ray how to wash and comb her hair, and she didn't cry. Only when they covered her hair with a cap did Ray say, "That must be what she sounds like when she cries," and she kept crying until the cap was off her head and out of sight.

By the time she was three months old, Callie had a mass of full silky curls that had once caused a woman to ask if I used pin curlers in her hair at night. That morning in Presque Isle, I'd combed the nine-month-old's hair into the style one friend referred to as "Callie's Jew-'fro," several inches of glossy black spirals through which you could just barely catch a glimpse of scalp near the spot at the back where she rubbed her head while fighting sleep.

The less blond of the housekeepers plunged her hand into Callie's hair, all the while telling my baby how darling she was. Callie smiled up at the woman, talking back to her as best she could. "Ma, ma, baba, da," she said. More than once, the housekeeper looked from the loose curls that slipped through her fingers to my dreadlocks and back, wondering, I assumed, how I came to have a daughter with hair so lustrous and fine.

My mother bristles when people comment on Callie's hair. "They've clearly never seen a black baby before," she says. "Black babies are born with hair."

She's right. Though the rule isn't universal. Some black babies are born bald and some white babies have lots of hair at the outset. It's not the science of racial differences in infant hair growth that intrigues me about my mother's reaction to people's responses to my daughter, but what her frustration reveals about her reactions to other people's expectations of beauty. It's as if my mother is annoyed that people are surprised to look into a black baby's stroller and find beauty. It's as if my mother is saying that she understands black beauty to be an original truth, and she is angered by people who have yet to acknowledge this reality. Sometimes I can't help but see where my mother is coming from, but if I thought like this all the time, I'd find the world a colder place. Usually I choose to believe people are simply overwhelmed not by the surprising beauty of a black baby but by the beauty of my *particular* child.

"I had hair just like hers when I was a baby," I said to the housekeeper. I have the photographs to prove it. "My mother says people used to tell her I should be a baby model, but she wanted me to have a normal life."

The women seemed to accept this comparative backstory as proof of maternity, and Callie and I and a couple extra bottles of hotel lotion were sent on our way. Into yet another normal day.

It was nearly ten a.m., and our ride to Fort Kent wouldn't arrive until one. Presque Isle published a self-guided walking tour online (I love historical tours) and I'd printed it before we left Oakland. Fortified by breakfast, I bundled Callie in her snowsuit, put her in the car seat, put the car seat in the stroller, covered her hands with mittens, pulled tight the snowsuit's hood, added two more blankets, pulled the car seat's canopy down to shield her from the wind, donned my parka, and headed down the half-mile hill into town.

THE AROOSTOOK RIVER and Presque Isle Stream form the peninsula that gave this town its current name. Before Dennis Fairbanks claimed the land in 1828, naming the town Fairbanks, the area was occupied by the Micmac, a nation from the Algonquin language group who lived along the northeastern Atlantic Seaboard southeast of the Gulf of Saint Lawrence and throughout the Maritime Provinces.

In 1838 and 1839, the area around Presque Isle was part of a territory dispute between the United States and Great Britain. The dispute, known unofficially as the Aroostook War—and even more unofficially as the Pork and Beans War—ended in 1842 with the signing of the agreement known officially as the Webster-Ashburton Treaty. United States Secretary of State Daniel Webster and British diplomat Alexander Baring, First Baron Ashburton, established the location of the Maine–New Brunswick border; established an agreement to share the use of the Great Lakes; reestablished a border at the forty-ninth parallel in the westward frontier; established the location of the border between Lake Superior and the Lake of the Woods that was originally, though somewhat ambiguously, defined in the 1783 Treaty of Paris; and called for direct American involvement in the suppression of the slave trade off the coast of Africa.

Let me repeat that last bit. A bloodless border skirmish between lumberjacks in far northeastern Maine (or southeastern New Brunswick, depending who you asked) led to a treaty that called for the United States to "effectually at once and for-ever" commit to curtailing the demand for African slaves.

A community with a nearly negligible black population had, as it turned out, played a very important role in the fate of black people all over the world.

With a population that is 95.4 percent white, Maine is the second whitest state in America. The county Callie and I were visiting, which is the size of the states of Rhode Island and Connecticut combined, has only about five hundred black residents. Largely because of all this whiteness, when I tell people I am visiting Maine, they invariably wonder about my reason. My reason is that, despite what a cursory look at demographics might suggest, Maine's history is my history, too.

Portland, Maine, for instance, is the site of the third-oldest black church still standing in America—the Abyssinian Meeting House, established in 1828 by abolitionists and formerly enslaved women and men. There are two things that are interesting to me about this fact. One is that Portland, Maine, once had a black population large enough to build and sustain a relatively substantial church. The second is that Maine has a population that remains interested enough in this aspect of its history to ensure that the building is still standing.

During the week, the Abyssinian Meeting House was the site of one of the first public schools for blacks in the country. In these and other ways, Maine established itself as a place where black people could find supportive communities, seek education, and build better lives. In 1826, two years before the founding of the Abyssinian Meeting House, John Brown Russwurm graduated from Bowdoin College in Brunswick, Maine. He was the third African American to graduate from a U.S. college. When Macon B. Allen completed the Maine bar exam in 1844, he became the first black person in America to pass a state bar. From 1866 to 1868, my own relative, John W. Dungy, a man formerly enslaved in Virginia, studied at Bates Seminary in Lewiston, Maine. But I wouldn't learn about this until later.

I did know, when I set out to explore Presque Isle, that Maine served a major role in the preamble to the Civil War, and I wanted to witness a part of this history with Callie.

Back in 2003, I paid a visit to my friend Matt O'Donnell in his house in Pittston, Maine. The point of the trip was to take a break from the book I was writing, a series of poems about African American life in Philadelphia and Virginia from 1830 to 1850. But writers never really take vacations from our obsessions. I must have mentioned my research at a social gathering, because during my visit I was taken on a tour of two buildings: a doctor's office that had once been a ship captain's home, and a house that was still a private residence. Both were located in Gardiner and in close proximity to the Kennebec River, which was once a major channel for hauling ice and other precious commodities. The homes had served as stops on the Underground Railroad.

The doctor's office had been remodeled so thoroughly that I could no longer see firsthand evidence of its role in the abolitionist network, but the private home still boasted a trapdoor in the attic over the L-shaped hallway that connected the house to its outbuildings. This trapdoor led to a crawl space where people escaping slavery, smuggled from the nearby river, were hidden until they could be safely transported farther north. The house stood on a quiet residential street in what appeared to be a guileless Maine town, but, crouching in that crawl space, I understood the state's role in American history in a more radical light.

It is almost as if the entire Civil War were started and ended by the people of Maine. While her husband professed at Bowdoin (about twenty-five miles south of the Underground Railroad sites I visited in Gardiner), Harriet Beecher Stowe wrote a significant portion of *Uncle Tom's Cabin*, first serialized in 1851. In the year of its publication, the novel outsold even the Holy Bible.

It is reported that Abraham Lincoln once called Stowe the little woman who started "this Great War," by which he meant the American Civil War. An interesting coincidence is that Joshua Chamberlain, a Bowdoin College professor like Stowe's husband, could be considered the man who ended the war. As a brigadier general, it was Chamberlain who accepted the surrender of arms of the Confederate Army of Northern Virginia on April 12, 1865, in Appomattox, Virginia, effectively ending major combat and, by commanding his men to salute the surrendering Confederate troops, setting an example of honor and forgiveness that would direct the course of Reconstruction.

Maine was heavily invested in the war and its outcome. Proportionally, the state committed more combatants to the conflict than any other state in the Union, as many as 80,000 men. Over 250 men came from Aroostook County, a sparsely and recently settled territory. With so many men engaged in combat, the state of Maine was destined to sustain heavy losses. On June 18, 1864, in Petersburg, Virginia, an ill-advised charge across an open field toward Confederate forces resulted in the death of more officers and men in a single day than was incurred by any other Union regiment in the war. At Petersburg, the First Maine Heavy Artillery Regiment lost 67 percent of its 900-man unit to death or severe injury. Though he survived that charge, the commanding officer, Colonel Daniel Chaplin, a merchant from Bangor, was later killed by a sharpshooter, thus joining his fate with those of the 681 men who died in combat or from disease during the First Maine's muster.

Sometimes these sorts of data points seem unconnected to the world in which I live. But when I study Maine's past, even the most quirky facts connect back to me. I get lost in the history, finding myself inside it.

•

HANNIBAL HAMLIN, whose son briefly served as an officer in the First Maine before being promoted to a significantly less fatal rank, served in the Aroostook War in 1839, a war whose key fort gave its name to the university at which I would speak later that evening.

In 1861, Hamlin was elected vice president of the United States under Abraham Lincoln, a post he would hold during the Civil War. Though Hamlin stayed in Bangor with his family for much of the conflict, and though he is reported to have called himself the least important man in Washington, Hamlin, like many of his fellow Mainers, helped to stir the pot that boiled over and brewed a war.

In Hamlin's day the Republican Party was America's radical, liberal party, and Hamlin was, in a substantial way, responsible for that. Formed in 1854 in opposition to the extension of slavery to Kansas and other free territories, the Republican Party of the 1850s and 1860s supported free enterprise and talked about protecting farmers and small businesses. Some things don't change. But by *free* the Republicans of the 1860s meant *not enslaved*. The Republican Party of the 1860s wanted to expand the free territories of the country, thus forcing the collapse of the system of slavery with which the average man could not compete. The farmers and businessmen they wanted to protect were yeomen farmers, craftsmen, and tradesmen whose small-scale output was no match for plantations and shops run on slave labor.

In 1860, there were about 4.5 million black people in America, roughly 3.7 million of whom were enslaved people residing in the Southern states. This might lead you to believe that the nation, particularly the South, was awash with white people who had direct access to this enormous unpaid labor force. In fact, this is far from the truth. Fewer than 2 percent of the entire U.S. population and just under 5 percent of the Southern population owned even one slave, and a significantly smaller percentage owned more than twenty. That means that the majority of America's slave labor force was controlled by a very small—but very powerful—minority. Consider that Jay Leno owns more than a hundred cars and John McCain more houses than he can count. When I visited Maine with my daughter, our family only owned one of the former and none of the latter. It happens like that in America, this unequal distribution of wealth. Hannibal Hamlin and his more radical supporters wanted to do something about that. The Civil War was as much about wealth distribution as it was about freeing black people from bondage. Though this capital—so unevenly distributed that it instigated a national feud we've yet to fully resolve—was derived from the lives and bodies of enslaved human beings.

Hamlin was part of the reason Maine was the first Northeastern state to join the Republican Party. In opposition to the 1854 signing of the Kansas-Nebraska Act, which repealed the Missouri Compromise and would allow slavery to migrate north and west to Kansas and other free territories, former U.S. Representative and then-Senator Hannibal Hamlin withdrew from the Democratic Party. He believed that the progression of slave economies into these new territories would make it harder for free enterprise to compete. As a Republican candidate for governor of Maine, he won a majority vote and was inaugurated in January 1857. Apparently preferring national politics to local, Hamlin withdrew from the office of governor later in the year and returned to the U.S. Senate, where he stayed until becoming Lincoln's VP.

Hamlin was selected as vice president because his presence in the cabinet created regional balance between the Northeast and the American West (represented by Lincoln). Lincoln had not met Hamlin before the election, and by many accounts didn't much care for him afterward. In order to achieve a different sort of cabinet balance for Lincoln's second term, the Republican

Party jettisoned Hamlin and chose, instead, a Southerner by the name of Andrew Johnson.

Hamlin's term in office expired on March 4, 1865. Thus, America was just forty days shy of having an anti-slavery president from Maine making decisions about the end of the Civil War and the implementation of Reconstruction. I daresay, the presence of Maine-born Hannibal Hamlin as vice president at the time of Lincoln's assassination, rather than the "Tennessee Tailor" Andrew Johnson, would have established a vastly different historical trajectory for the United States.

•

I WAS CONFRONTED BY the notion of alternative histories as I pushed Callie's stroller through Presque Isle.

If the Pork and Beans War had turned out otherwise and it was Britain who got these 7,015 square miles of contested territory, the day's stroll might have been undertaken in Canada, and the received history of white settlement in this part of Aroostook County might have less to do with the War Between the States and more to do with Peter Bull, who came to this area from New Brunswick in 1819 to set up a sawmill.

Mostly gone from the accounts are Bull's name, the names of the twenty or so other families who settled the area around the same time, and the individual identities of the Micmac who named the river and once called all the land around it home. History is little more than a record of disputed erasures. It was an American, Fairbanks, whose claim on this land was recognized, but even his name was pushed aside by 1859 when the incorporated township officially dubbed itself Presque Isle.

It looked like the baby was sleeping. The sun beat through the clouds, so the March day was warming. I pushed her stroller as the walking tour's map directed. Past a wool carding mill, lumber mills, a grist mill, several mansions, a furniture factory, a tinware factory, a grange, and halls where the Masons, the Odd Fellows, the Knights of Pythias, and members of the Women's Christian Temperance Union could meet. The baby and I strolled past the substantial home of James Phair, postmaster, hotelier, and brother of the "Starch King" Thomas H. Phair, who owned twenty of the sixty-two area starch factories. Potatoes were the crop of the land, but without reliable roads, Aroostook County farmers took to selling their product to these starch factories, converting a perishable product into a marketable resource. In 1894, James Phair sold his hotel to the railroad company to make room for the train station that the potato brought to Presque Isle, and with that railroad line came the promise of more wealth.

But much of what the potato built was no longer there for us to see. Fires, including the "Big Fire of 1883," destroyed much of Main Street and ravished the wooden buildings and boardwalks of the town. Major railroad lines and shipping channels and interstates and airline routes all flirted with Presque Isle, but then passed it by, while a potato blight crippled the cash crop, and starched collars became a thing of the past.

I pushed the stroller through the old downtown district, and turned right onto Church Street, where I stopped in front of the white-columned Presque Isle Congregational Church, pastored, for six months in 1879, by Harriet Beecher Stowe's son Charles "Charley" Stowe. There I discovered, via an informative plaque, that the building where Charley Stowe preached was gone.

This new building, larger than the original, replaced the first one, which burned in 1909.

It was snowing by this time, the first snow Callie had ever experienced, but bundled in her snowsuit and blanket, with a hood and oversized mittens, she looked completely disinterested in the picture I snapped in front of the church. As if, despite all the connections I'd discovered, nothing we'd experienced mattered to her.

•

IN ONE OF OUR CORRESPONDENCES about the details of my trip, the woman who invited me to speak at Fort Kent recommended we visit Main Street's Café Sorpreso during our Presque Isle layover, but Callie and I had been delayed leaving the hotel, and I'd taken my time on our tour through town, so now we didn't have the leisure to sit. What I did, instead, was duck into Governor's Restaurant for take-away.

But nothing happened quickly while we were in Presque Isle.

I often found it easier to carry Callie's stroller up a set of stairs than to push her to Saturn and back on some long, windy access ramp, but the stairs at Governor's Restaurant were crowded with patrons.

Soon the ramp, too, was crowded with patrons.

These new patrons stopped to look into the stroller. "Isn't she a doll!" one said.

"Would you look at all that hair!" said another. Even with a hood, Callie displayed quite a crown.

A third woman wore a coat emblazoned with the local campus's logo: THE UNIVERSITY OF MAINE AT PRESQUE ISLE—NORTH OF ORDINARY. "Would you look at those eyes?" the woman said. "I bet she doesn't miss a beat, does she?"

The women asked, "Where are you visiting from?" "How are you liking Maine?" "What do you think of all this snow?"

The first woman asked, "How long do you plan on staying in Presque Isle?"

I smiled. I said, "Thank you." I said, "It's a lovely town, but I'm just here for the morning." The three kept peering into the stroller, smiling at me, then peering into the stroller again, as if Callie and I were an inconceivable anomaly. I said, "I better get the baby out of the cold."

Inside the restaurant, I ordered a lobster roll. I ordered a whoopie pie, too, because there was no one there to tell me I shouldn't. I love these Maine treats. Their dark chocolate-cake-like cookies surrounding marshmallow cream fillings always seem like a good idea at the outset.

After I'd placed my order, I waited on the bench in the restaurant's foyer, rocking the stroller and trying to read a real estate brochure, curious what it would be like to live in a place where property was so cheap. I retracted the stroller's canopy and removed the snowsuit's hood so Callie wouldn't overheat.

"Would you look at that baby?" said the hostess.

"Have you ever seen so much hair on a baby before?" asked a patron.

"You're not letting her get cold, are you?" asked somebody's grandmother.

"Were you on the plane with my boyfriend last night?" asked a young waitress who'd rounded the corner and cut through the crowd. By this time I'd put down the real estate brochure and was free to focus on the wall of words that was coming my way. "Driving home from the airport, my boyfriend told me all about this baby who flew in the seat next to him. He said she was really sweet, so quiet." She said this as if Callie's calmness in the restaurant explained how she knew my baby was *the* baby her boyfriend had come to admire. "He must have told me three times that he wished we'd gone back inside the airport so I could see her. This is that baby, right? Cute as a button. Cute as can be. He told me she was a darling." The waitress smiled into Callie's stroller, tickling the top of her snowsuit in a manner that made it look like she had chucked the baby under the chin. "I can't believe my luck, bumping into you like this," she said. "I was just in the kitchen dropping an order and one of the waitresses told me there was a cute little baby out here I had to see. I can't believe it's the same baby my boyfriend told me about last night. He said she was the sweetest baby he'd ever flown with in all his life."

"How's that puppy of yours?" I asked, remembering her boyfriend had bought her a Lab because he thought she needed company while he was away working oil rigs off the coast of Louisiana.

"Oh." She smiled. "She's the sweetest little thing in the

world." She tapped Callie's snowsuit again and started to turn away. "I can't wait to tell him you came into the restaurant. What are the odds of running into you this way?" She headed back to her tables.

"One lobster roll," the cashier called.

I grabbed the sandwich and tossed my black and white treat into the brown paper bag.

The route back to our hotel was steeper than I'd remembered, and I ended up trudging uphill in as close to a jog as I could muster wearing boots and a parka and pushing thirty pounds of baby and stroller. Callie had fallen back to sleep, cozy and protected from the biting snow. Rounding the corner into the driveway of the Presque Isle Inn & Convention Center at about 1:10, I saw an official-looking vehicle with a woman standing by it, smiling and waving in my direction.

"Hi! I'm Lisa. I'm the student who's gonna drive you up to UMFK," the woman said.

I paused near the rear of the car long enough to catch my breath and tell her I had to run into the hotel to go to the bathroom, change the baby, and collect our things from the bell stand. "Actually, it might be a little while. I should feed her, too," I said.

"Oh, no problem. I'm happy to wait as long as you need. I'm just glad I found you," said Lisa. She helped me haul the stroller up the five stairs leading to the lobby. "My cell phone battery died, and I wasn't sure how we'd make contact when I got here," she said, settling into one of the upholstered chairs to wait. "But I shouldn't have worried." She sighed, clearly comfortable in the place where she sat. "I spotted you two right away."

WRITING HOME

When I was a girl-child, home was a street called Bluff View, the uppermost block in a terraced neighborhood of Southern Californian houses. In the summer, when I was young and untired and forced to bed before the sun went down, my lullaby was the view my bedroom window afforded of the hills behind my house. Desert oak, prickly pear, eucalyptus, sage: I fell asleep cataloging this place. In the daytime, I would scramble over one bluff and up the hill behind it, playing teacher in the caves my neighbors and I found, scratching lessons in the chalky sand that lined the walls. We played doctor with stethoscopes fashioned from rocks and the necklaced stalks of wild mustard. We knew the contours and passages of those hills like we knew the halls and classrooms of our other, inside, school. Walking down a slope is different than walking on flat land, and each part of my legs recorded required positions until they could move as correctly up and down those bluffs as my tongue might move over the alphabet. My body memorized its place in those hills.

But even while I lived at the center of everything I knew, everything I knew erased itself. Before I entered high school, construction had begun on summit estates for our town's growing mogul class. The hilltop was leveled and two of my favorite caves were lost. From my bedroom window I could now see the red tile roof of the pizza king's palacio. Less desert oak. A weaker scent of sage. When my parents bought the house on Bluff View, our backyard marked the edge of human landscaping. It was not uncommon to find tumbleweed resting in our lounge chairs, to leave wild poppies blooming along the margins of cut grass. Now the hills were asphalt and ice plant. The wild dogs we called coyotes moved down into our backyards, fighting with raccoons over scraps from overturned trash cans and preying on small pets.

Development in California means the building of homes, the imposition of landscaping, the digging of pools. Development in California means controlling what exists and creating something new, something only the diversion of rivers for the maintenance of reservoirs can sustain. Development in California means the mass irrigation of newly planted lawns. Houses, houses everywhere and not a wild mustard field to see. Not even the acres of organized agriculture that first moneyed the region survive. The City of Orange in Orange County kept an orange tree in a fenced area, a skinny-branched specimen saved to represent the fields for which the region was named. I grew up on a street called Bluff View in the midst of California's ambition for development. When I write about nature, I am writing about loss. I am writing about discovering home where home has been replaced by structures I do not want to recognize. The place I was born into no longer exists. I don't have a town I can call home. Unless language is home. Unless, when I write, what had slipped away is found.

Once, I knew the silence and wind-cry of my California hills. In California, the sky speaks with a clipped tongue. Mountains shoulder into the conversation, the ocean sighs in frustration, and that frustration rolls over us, is fog. Say the sky and the sea have been arguing all night. Say the mountain blanketed itself and withdrew into silence but the sky and the sea kept at it through the night. Say it is finally morning. When the ocean rolls its wave-blue eyes and sighs, no one will believe the bright points the sky still holds on to. When I lived in California, I was at home in the language of sky and mountaintop and sea. But what my parents came to California to find began to slip away and we moved away as well.

I found myself in Iowa and believed for a long time that I had lost my home. The language of place is a slow speech to learn. Iowa is blue uninterrupted, blue talking all day and a darker blue still talking through the night. Just the waist-high tips of new corn there to listen, and they not saying anything, only nodding their young heads. A new language. I moved to Iowa and didn't write for months. When a poem finally came, it was written in a different tongue.

Now it is half my lifetime since I lived on Bluff View, and I have traveled enough and moved enough to know that home is not a place. I am thinking perhaps home is not language, either. Language is too easy to lose. Perhaps home is memory.

It is years later and I am a traveler, walking. I am on public land: a park, a knoll, a meadow. I am glad to own the memories I own and through those memories to belong someplace, to have some place belong to me. I am remembering, and I am writing a poem in my many tongues. A poem having to do with comfort; something having to do with peace. Then a dog comes growling toward me. A dog with still tail and pointed ears. A dog with fanged mouth and purposeful eyes.

The sky is quiet, and the dog is barking, and someone the dog trusts and will obey says, *Sic her, sic.*

If memory is home, I am a long way from hope. I have escaped and am running. I have to remember what has been said: I am black and female; no place is for my pleasure. How do I write about the land and my place in it without these memories: the runaway with the hounds at her heels; the complaint of the poplar at the man-cry of its load; land a thing to work but not to own? How do I write about the land and my place in it without remembering, without shaping my words around, the history I belong to, the history that belongs to me? The dog drags me to fields of memory where I toil from can see to can't. What I write about the land and my place in it is informed by this fact: Sometimes the landscape is of little comfort. Sometimes I want to run far away from home.

When I was a child in the hills behind the street called Bluff View, I knew no threat nor fear. Development, the advancement of possession, had not pushed coyotes from the hillside into our backyards. My poems are informed by displacement and oppression, but they are also informed by peace, by self-possession. When I was a child on Bluff View, the dogs we call bloodhounds, the slave trackers' tool, were nothing I knew to remember. I was a girl-child in that kingdom of open space, and all the land I could see and name and touch was mine to love. No one, no thing, possessed another, nothing was developed apart from my heart. When I was a child in the hills behind the street called Bluff View, there was no such thing as history. Sometimes my poems rest again in that quiet space, that comfort.

The dog is closer. A woman repeats her command, but it is something altogether different this time.

Sit, girl. Sit.

BOUNDS

——

1

This morning, while I was braiding her hair, Callie worked on singing "Twinkle, Twinkle, Little Star," a song she's been mastering for several weeks. She gets better at it, and then, by some gauges, she gets worse. Someday soon she'll be a genius at "Twinkle, Twinkle, Little Star," and because I've been watching her incremental progress, I will either quietly delight in the accomplishment or I will nonchalantly say to Ray, "Oh, you haven't heard her sing that song? She's been doing that for a while."

It's like the jumping she's been practicing. She spent part of Saturday morning climbing up the ledge on the Fairyland lawn stage and asking me to lift her off, to help her fly to the ground. The space between the proscenium and the grass is about two and a half feet. It doesn't look like a steep drop to me, until I imagine preparing to jump the same length as my body is tall. I would hesitate if such a leap were before me. Why shouldn't she hesitate? I didn't push her to do any more than she was ready to do, but when the three-year-old guests from the birthday party we were attending swarmed the stage and started jumping to the grass below, twenty-two-month-old Callie thought maybe she could jump, too.

She couldn't jump yet. She actually didn't understand the physical components of the jump, and so she wanted me to hold her hands while she practiced the motions required for the fall. When she got up her nerve, she took what amounted to an exaggerated step off the ledge. One foot prepared to lead and, as I supported her weight, she mustered her will and allowed the other foot to follow. Soon enough she wanted to take these big steps on her own, and she shunned me, pulling her hands away with determination and walking briskly off the ledge.

Watching this process gave me a new understanding of the concept of taking a giant step. These leaps of faith our lives demand of us. Callie, not even two years old, often has to master her fears and lack of physical knowledge in order to do things she needs to do, like move a cup to her mouth without spilling the contents down her front. She's got to be even more in control to do the things she *wants* to do, like leaping off a ledge that's higher than she is tall. She has no inclination to limit herself, and I try to reduce the limits that might be placed upon her. She could have been stuck back at the bottom of the hill, sitting by the red wagon that none of the older party guests were playing with anymore. Instead, there she was, teaching herself to jump.

This time last year, she was touching grass for the very first time, and that, too, was new territory. We'd taken her to the

Fairyland Easter show to see the tap-dancing bunnies—six adults in costume tuxedos and bunny ears tapping their way across the stage, simultaneously delighting and baffling their young audience. After the show, we'd taken Callie behind the main stage's building to sit on the proscenium that overlooked a wide expanse of lawn. Callie nursed in the relative quiet of that green space, and when she finished, we put her down on the spring grass so she could crawl freely.

Her hand settled down as it might on a blanket, then flew up as if she had touched something offensive, something frightening. She expressed more surprise upon first contact with the grass than she had the whole time the enormous bunnies had been hopping around the stage.

Fairyland is a multi-acre, storybook-focused amusement park, but Callie was never hesitant about encountering an eight-foot-tall, bubble-blowing dragon or working her way into the singing mouth of Willie the Whale. To my daughter, the mysteries of Fairyland seemed par for the course. When she was on the grass, though, her expression suggested that the lawn was prickly and somewhat cruel. She reached up so I could lift her away from the offensive sensation. When I didn't, she pushed herself beyond her initial discomfort and tested the grass again. The grass seemed to grow soft under her hands, then tickly. Her face moved from horror to delight. Even when she discovered new things about and in the grass, she never fully settled back into horror.

I was thinking of that as I watched Callie teach herself to jump off the ledge. Just last year, for the first time in her ten months on the planet, she was rolling around in grass she'd been at first afraid to touch. I want to consider my daughter's learning curve in the same ways I might consider my own interactions with the unknowns of the world. How much fuller her experiences are when she reaches toward the unknown! Encounters with people and places and things that are new to her, these are the experiences around which her life will be constructed. Just last year, she was barely crawling. Now she's pushing herself off the safety of a stable surface and onto the grass far below. Now she is learning to fly.

•

SHE GOT PRETTY GOOD at jumping last Saturday at Fairyland, but yesterday was Thursday. And Thursday was a whole new day.

We were about to enter the University of San Francisco's library, where Callie would have to sit quietly with a stack of toys while I gave a poetry reading. The man who'd invited me to read to the USF poetry club is the father of two. When I wrote to say the child care I'd arranged for the afternoon had fallen through, he encouraged me to bring Callie with me.

Usually when I read in the Bay Area, I'll leave Callie with a family member or a local sitter. If I bring her along, I'll ask someone positioned at the back of the room—a student or a fellow poet—to hold her for the brief time I'm onstage. My host offered to be such a minder. "I only have boys," he insisted. "It will be a delight to look after a girl."

This would be a longer reading than I'd ever done with my daughter in attendance and we'd be inside a library, so her presence would be audible if she started acting up. She's nearly two, I reasoned. She could self-entertain for a while. Callie would be a good girl if I provided the proper distractions, I reassured myself. Because the behavior of a child is often seen as a reflection of the quality of the mother, I worried that things might go poorly. "Do you need to get your zoomies out before we go inside?" I asked her.

She slithered out of my arms and began running around the two-ton bronze wolves that guarded the USF library. Installed on the campus just six months before our visit, the castings represented the university's lineage from Iñigo López de Loyola, whose family crest sported a couple of well-fed wolves. But what did Callie care of the history of the statues, the history of the 160-year-old university that hosted us, the history of the 470-year-old Society of Jesus that founded it, the history of Jesus, the history of wolves? All she seemed to care about was what she could do with her own body. Callie patted the hard, cool bronze, sounding her voice into the drum of the wolves' bellies. "Woof! Woof! Woof!" she cried.

Leading to the wolves was a lawn terraced by a series of concrete ledges, each with a swatch of grass waiting two feet below. After she'd tired of trying to climb up the backs of the colossal wolves, Callie toddled in the direction of the concrete ledges and learned to jump all over again.

First she touched the grass, coming to understand it as an ally. Then she climbed onto a slab of concrete, held my hands, and let me help her fly. Then she walked herself off the ledge, as if horizontal movement could defy gravity. It was like watching a Road Runner cartoon—that brief moment of suspension before the brain kicks in and the body falls. After gravity had won again and again, Callie let go of her dependence on horizontal motion. She launched off both feet at once—she took a little jump and went down with a giggle.

Her learning curve took about thirty minutes. If we do it again later this week, it might take fifteen. Repeated experience collapses the amount of time it takes her to learn new tasks. Who knows how long it will be before Callie simply jumps, without all the preliminaries? When she does, will I remember all the work it took for her to master that basic and necessary skill?

•

THIS MORNING'S "Twinkle, Twinkle, Little Star" went something like, "Inkle inkle hum hum star hum are hum up a hum high high hum star hum hum high." The rhythm was completely off, which distressed me because one of Callie's superpowers has been an incredible memory for melodies.

I first realized that she knew the song when I was singing it to her and she began to hum along. I stopped singing because I was shocked to hear her hum so well, but she continued to hum the whole measure, getting the tune right note for note. I was sad to realize that the song was yet another thing she'd learned at the day care we'd enrolled her in a few months before. But I let go of that sadness and enjoyed, instead, my daughter's musical memory.

Over time, her mastery of the tune grew so well that last week I recorded our duet, mother singing the words and daughter humming along like a harmonica accompanist. She never missed a beat. Her pitch was perfect. Perhaps my excitement was out of proportion to the nature of her accomplishments but, listening to Callie, I suffered the sin of pride.

Katherine Ellison, the author of *The Mommy Brain*, claims that 73 percent of new mothers express outsized pride in their babies. We do this, she argues, because the survival of our offspring depends on our neurochemical engagement in that child's success. I know Callie is learning because that is what her brain is tracked to do, but my investment in her demands all my resources. To remain this fully committed, I have to believe in myself as much as I believe in her.

When she wants to sing the song, my little twenty-two-month-old says, "Up a!" and catches my eye.

"Twinkle, twinkle . . ." I begin, and she hums along.

Not long ago, she started adding words. The humming began to be punctuated with an occasional "high" or "star" in addition to "up a" and "inkle," but always the pitch and the rhythm were right.

But this morning, it fell apart. It was as if all she wanted to do was get at the power words in the song. She must have said "high" five times when working through the lyrics, which messed up the rhythm entirely. I tried to sing the whole piece to help her along, or rather, to help her return to her previous level of mastery, but she covered her mouth with a finger and said, "Shhh. Shhh." Then she started to sing again, and this time it was even worse. "Inkle inkle ittle high up a high I'm a high inkle are high." The tune was barely recognizable, though the words were getting clearer every time.

Callie is getting very close to cracking the code of language. Or, I suppose I should say that Callie is getting very close to cracking *a* code of language, because there will be plenty more mysteries of language that will reveal themselves over time.

Language has always brought, to me, experiences of both triumph and torture.

I was sixteen before I grasped the power of abstract language—riding home from high school with my friend Todd, who had a pet chameleon. We had that in common. When I was four, my family lived in Nigeria while my father was a UNICEF consultant to the Nigerian government, supporting the implementation of basic health systems. The groundskeeper in the park near the compound where we stayed captured chameleons for my sister and me. We used ropes for leashes and treated the creatures as pets. I was telling Todd about how we'd created a sense of intimacy with the reptiles. "Kathryn named them," I told him, because that was my understanding of the source of their names. "She named one of them after me! It was really sweet of her. They were so cute—we really loved them. Their names were Camille and—"

I stopped midsentence. For the first time, I realized that what I'd perceived as an act of generosity on my sister's part was simply a play on words. Camille and Leon. How absurd to think my sister, or those captive creatures, cared about me. I wasn't being honored with a namesake. If anything, the names compared me to a reptile. I'd seen myself at the center of something special that now was nothing but a pun. Language fell apart for me after that. I spent more time parsing phrases, looking for trapdoors. I had moved into a new kind of thinking.

According to the psychologist Jean Piaget, when I kept Camille and Leon as pets my four-year-old thoughts were ruled by my "Preoperational" mind. My sister (eight at the time) was already moving toward "Concrete Operational Thinking." She could conceive of reverse operational structures: Camille is my sister; this creature is a chameleon; part of this creature's name sounds like my sister's. She could move toward a form of inductive logic: Camille is my sister's name but, since the name Camille also sounds like part of the word chameleon, it is fun that this chameleon is named Camille. Her appreciation of wordplay may not have taken me into account in any intentional way.

At four, according to Piaget, I thought more egocentrically, less aware that there were realities beyond my own perspective, and I focused on one problem at a time, unable to manipulate all the intuitive comprehensions the pun on the word chameleon required. By the time I related the story to Todd, my mode of ideation was moving (albeit somewhat fitfully) toward what Piaget would call the "Formal Operational Stage." The teacher and blogger Shawn Cornally writes about his efforts to make math more intelligible to high school students, who are going through the same sort of mental developments I was dealing with during my conversation with Todd. In an article titled "Teenagers and Abstract Thinking: Unclear on the Concept?" Cornally writes, "Abstraction is the ability to simultaneously consider multiple states of a system in order to analyze it for patterns, behavior, and predictability." During adolescence, young people move at different rates into this ability to think abstractly, and the ability to abstractly conceptualize information that was initially received during more concrete phases of intellectual development is sometimes delayed. The information was originally concretely filed in what is essentially a different person's mind, these theories suggest. Repeating the names of my pet chameleons in the company of another, hearing them as a stranger would hear them, I recognized for the first time that those names represented a variety of perspectives that had, hitherto, been unavailable to me. "I've been saying our pet chameleons' names my whole life, and I've never heard them like that before," I told Todd.

So I will not say that Callie, at twenty-two months, is about to crack all the codes that language has to offer. She's only just moving out of Piaget's "Sensorimotor Stage," when children synthesize their understanding of the world through senses rather than through language. It is, in fact, her rapid accrual of language that will jettison her out of this first stage of human intellectual development and into the next. Or perhaps it's the movement from one stage to the next that triggers the rapid development of language. Or perhaps Piaget's theories, as some would argue, aren't accurate appraisals of cognitive development. Many of Piaget's notions were established by watching his own children and their friends—hardly a broad or diverse study group—and Piaget himself would admit his theories don't manifest in all individuals and all cases as an unvarying path. Perhaps these theories haven't been accurately translated. I discovered, for instance, nearly thirty years after my conversation with Todd and some time after originally writing this essay, that it hadn't been my sister who named our chameleons. My father named them—with no thought to the possibility that as a result I would formulate understandings both about early childhood development and the security of my relationship with my sister. So, who can say whether or to what degree Piaget's observations apply? What I can say with certainty is that Callie is beginning to understand the power of language, and she is exercising that power a little more every day.

•

For over a month she has been able to identify zeros. Any O-shaped object is a "zero." So the sentence I am writing now, with 100 in the middle, would contain seven zeros. A few weeks after she nailed zero, she began to recognize the number 8. Perhaps it's the double-0 factor that enabled that. Then, during our trip to Chico last week, she stood in the elevator bay on the second floor of the Hotel Diamond and pointed to the numeral on the lintel. "Two!"

Callie understands that certain symbols are connected to certain sounds. And she can count to two, so that particular number has a conceptual meaning to her as well. She is beginning to pair symbols with words and words with concepts. She's beginning, in other words, to demonstrate a mind I can recognize.

Tracy Butts, a faculty member at Cal State, Chico, watched Callie while I visited a poetry class. We'd not been with Tracy for more than ten minutes before Callie reached out to invite her embrace. She's a little diplomatic liaison, going along with me to win hearts and minds. Sometimes the heart and mind that need winning are my own. Leaving her with strangers requires blind optimism on my part, wherein I must assume the people we encounter are intrinsically good. My baby's willingness to be left with strangers, her willingness to go to strangers, and the goodness I read on these people's faces when they are holding her—these help me relinquish a great deal of what otherwise might be unmitigated terror.

My host and I walked out of Tracy's office, and Callie started to cry. It wasn't a panicked cry. It was more of a grumble. In the same way she's learning to speak English, her father and I are learning to understand the only language she has full command of right now. I said to my host, "She's just registering her complaint that I've left. She'll stop crying in a minute," and before we were fifty yards down the hall, she did.

Later, we learned a student had walked by Tracy's door wearing a backpack. "Backpack," Callie said, distracted from the dissatisfaction that had brought her to tears and delighted, instead, by her ability to identify a familiar object. Tracy said she took the baby outside to play on the grass, near the stairs. The blue jays flitted above her, and the baby said, "Bird." The dogwoods were budding, the azaleas were in full bloom, and the baby wanted to touch all the flowers. She seemed to approve of the energy on the college campus. "Backpack! Backpack! Backpack!" Tracy said she said.

Right now, words are clusters of sound. Or words are labels, sounds that connect to a thing. She hasn't yet articulated words that represent a state of mind. When I left Tracy's office, Callie didn't yell, *Stop! I want you to come back!* She has *baby, boots, brush*—I just heard that this morning as I was doing her hair. She has *lamb, cat, dog, horse, cow.* When she says "woof" rather than "wolf," she is using the animal's sound to identify it. Nouns facilitate actions, and the few action words she's articulated have facilitated nouns. If she says *moo,* I will hand her the toy cow. She doesn't need language to identify desire quite yet because a simple naming of an object is enough to get her desires fulfilled. Why say, "I am thirsty," when simply saying "milk" will solve the problem? Why say anything but "backpack" if that word alone will get her out of an unfamiliar office and into the more familiar embrace of the grass and flowers and stairs on a campus quad?

But new words are creeping in. *Hot* is one of her favorites when it comes to food, and also to the area around the oven. *Shhh* means she would like to sing by herself or hear the person on the radio do the singing without her mother's interference, or it could mean that she's tired and wants quiet so she can go to sleep more peacefully. *Stop* means, *Don't tickle me anymore, or Don't comb my hair, or Don't put on that lotion: I am physically uncomfortable, and this immediate discomfort is your fault.* She is still organizing her thoughts through sensation. Her desire to halt an uncomfortable physical sensation (a touch, or a sound—which scientists might argue is actually just another form of a touch, sound waves entering her ear and *touching* the proper receptors) has inspired her first articulations of state-of-being words and preliminary action verbs. As these begin to multiply, will she move through the world very differently than she has been doing thus far?

I am devoting more attention than I can ever remember devoting to trying to understand the experiences of another human being, and still I can't fully inhabit her mind. When she sings "Twinkle, Twinkle, Little Star," does she understand that it is a song about a star far out in space and the great mystery around what that star is and what it does and why it looks like a diamond? She does not. Not now. But one day she will.

How long until that day?

Only a month ago, driving over the MacArthur Maze with the baby in the backseat and her favorite CD on a loop, I grew up a little more. "So- nay- la- latina. So- nay- la- latina," I sang along, until I realized—with accident-inviting horror—that I'd always sung that verse as a sort of gibberish inflected by my Southern Californian, Spanglish-infused upbringing. What I should have been singing all these years was the French phrase, "Sonnez la matinée"—sounds that had no meaning to me in my youth.

Until yesterday, Callie was basically just singing musical notes, but this morning she was trying to work with language. She's about to take a flying leap, my girl.

2

THE WORD *BOUND* means several different things, and when I think of my daughter, I think of all of them, simultaneously and, also, discretely.

To bound means to leap forward, as in, *Callie's development is progressing by leaps and bounds.* That definition implies rapid forward motion with upward mobility as part of its intent. If it is likely that something will happen (Callie will learn to speak in full sentences, Callie will learn ballet, Callie will go to college one day), we say, *It is bound to happen.* But if something is tied up and restricted (say, our financial situation makes it impossible for us to pay her college tuition), we might lament, *The poor thing has been root-bound.* Just as bound implies exuberant forward movement, it also indicates restraint. *It is beyond the bounds of Callie's imagination to understand that the little star that twinkles in the sky is actually the light from blazing gases that may have been traveling toward us for millions of years.* Bound is a limiting value. The edge of possibility. The territorial boundary beyond which we cannot now, and maybe cannot ever, extend. In bounds. Out of bounds. Legal, appropriate, acceptable. Or not.

Though we ought not forget the word's entanglement with the horrors of perpetual servitude that are a part of our history, to be bound is not necessarily a bad thing. *We have leather-bound books in the house. Yesterday, I combed her hair and bound it in Goody® Ouchless® Elastics.* To bind something can simply mean to wrap it up: sometimes for safety, sometimes for beauty, sometimes for ease.

I bound myself to your father, and he bound himself to me, and now that we have you, daughter, we are both bound to thee. To be bound up in someone or something is to be focused on that person or thing to the exclusion of all others, which is how I often feel when I am in Callie's company.

I am a writer. I think about language every day. And now I am bound to someone for whom language is, daily, a new invention. *Bound* means heading somewhere, as I am often doing with Callie—as I am, perhaps, always doing with Callie. *We're on a plane bound for Vermont*, I could say.

·

"DADDY COFFEE," she said when she saw me with a mug this morning.

"Mommy doesn't drink coffee, Sweet Pea. This is tea."

"Mommy tea," she said, pointing at my steaming mug.

I would find this labeling endearing in any circumstance, but it was particularly interesting to me today because we are not anywhere near Daddy or his coffee. It has been just over a week since our jumping lessons on the Fairyland proscenium. I've brought Callie with me to Vermont, and we were eating breakfast in my sister's South Burlington kitchen while I prepared to drive ninety minutes to talk about nature poetry with college students in a place called Craftsbury Common. We're 3,012 miles away from our Oakland, California, home, with a relative she's only met six times in her life. Yet Callie seemed unperturbed by the change in her circumstances, happily identifying the familiar objects in her environment.

During our trip yesterday, we saw the space shuttle *Discovery* parked on Dulles Airport's tarmac, awaiting its final transfer to the Smithsonian museum. What dumb luck had us sitting on the right side of the plane to see this slice of history?

The *Discovery* rested on the back of a modified Boeing 747, looking rather like the smaller of a pair of mating mantises.

Callie flies on at least two airplanes a month. That technology is part of the fabric of her daily life. She can recognize the sound of an airplane as it passes over, differentiating the buzz of a jet plane from the whir of a helicopter. Airplanes are familiar, utilitarian, and nameable. Callie pointed toward the space shuttle that was, even as it sat before us, obsolete. "Airplane," she said, noting the more familiar Boeing jet first. "Baby airplane," she said, acknowledging its burden, the *Discovery*, in the language she had at her disposal.

·

I T WASN'T UNTIL we'd boarded our return flight that I realized it would be the final solo trip I'd take with Callie as a lap child. She's growing too big. There will be more flights, but the round-trip to Vermont was the last one I will ever make with my daughter sitting in my lap. She's halfway through her twenty-second month, and her legs reach nearly to the seat back in front of us. Her twenty-five pounds numb my thighs after a while. Another one of the lovely and difficult experiences of motherhood is drawing to an end.

I remembered a woman I sat next to on my way home from an Associated Writing Programs Conference in Chicago. This was a year before I'd thought to invite Callie into my womb. I had not yet constructed myself as a mother, didn't yet command the expansiveness the role demands. I was flying standby to get back to Ray as quickly as possible, and I was handed the very worst seat on the plane. *Beggars can't be choosers*, I told myself, as I was directed to a seat in the last row before the lavatories, between a dour woman in the window seat and a very large woman who was dangling a very large lap child into the aisle.

The boy kicked and squirmed and protested being held for three and a half hours. In an effort to soothe him, the mother fed the boy apple juice and cookies. "Calm down," she'd tell him. "Stop kicking," she'd say. The boy kicked some more.

He kicked my calf. He kicked the seat in front of him. He kicked my thigh. He raised his arm to wipe his runny nose and slammed his fist into my arm as he returned it to his side. Sometimes his mother tried to wipe his nose. In response, the boy hit her arm away. The smack of his chubby hand against his mother's chubby forearm sounded like raw meat slapped down on a butcher's block.

"We're taking the train from now on," the mother told her boy. "You could run around if we were on the train."

I was merciless toward that woman. I was merciless toward that child. I wanted to throw the sugary apple juice away. I wanted to banish the cookies. I wished they'd come up with the train scheme before I'd had the misfortune of squeezing into their row. When I arrived home, I wrote a letter to the airline complaining about the large woman and her large lap child. When I say I was merciless, I mean to say I was petty, judgmental, self-involved, shortsighted, and cruel.

What I deserve for my lack of mercy is a merciless seatmate on every flight I take with my lap child. This is a world in which some children—particularly children born to certain bodies—are written off as hopeless before they've even learned to speak for themselves. My child could easily become the focus of such derision. What I deserve for the times I've dismissed other people's children is blind reciprocity for my disdain. Instead, dumb luck gets us people like the chief of staff of the Northern California VA who sat beside us on our flight home from Vermont. As he eyed my daughter with nostalgic delight, this father of four said, "Babies are evolutionarily programmed to be cute." By the middle of the flight, Callie was trammeling his slacks under her little shoes, playing with the lights over his head, and sitting on his wife's lap, opening and shutting the window shade. Somewhere between Cleveland and San Francisco, a flight attendant brought Callie a cookie straight from the first-class oven. "You see?" said the doctor. "If something happens to the parents, babies need to be cute enough that other adults will want to take care of them."

The word *change* means: to make or become different, to transform (into a different substance or thing), to move from one phase to another, to arrive at a fresh position. As in, *The circumstances may change.* As in, *The mother must change.*

When Callie was about one month old, she would stare into my eyes for long stretches of time. They write love scenes like this into movies. There's language for the feeling her gaze stirred in me, but the words are insufficient for the magnitude of my experience. I'd changed from a woman who thought very little of babies to a woman who thought of little else.

When she was six months old and would wrap her small hands around the back of my head, pulling me toward her, she would make as if to eat me. "I love you! I love you! I love you!" we would say when kissing her, and it felt as if her kisses were saying that, too. She devoured the third eye on our foreheads. We thought that must be what our kisses felt like to her, our mouths so huge that our little pecks consumed entire portions of her face. Those long gazes in the first month, the consuming kisses in the sixth, they changed me.

They changed my idea of scale. I saw how large I was by comparison. Physically, as well as emotionally. My ideas were larger than they used to be. My fears. They changed my ideas about repetition. Things repeated themselves, and I needed them to. I grew impatient for expressions of love from her. I wanted to experience them again and again, and I understood these repeat-worthy expressions in terms I would not have understood before. I saw patterns in the rest of the world, too. Repetitions I'd not bothered to notice before. I sought patterns in music, in clothing, in literature. Research shows that mothers' brains light up—of course they light up!—when a baby smiles. But people will tell you—repeatedly—it's just gas that turns the baby's mouth up. Faced with these notions, maybe your recurring hunger for these smiles would change. Mine did not.

I changed her diapers as many as eight times in an hour, but even after cleaning up her constant shit, how much I loved her did not change. Or, if it changed, it was only because my love grew stronger in the dispensation of these ministrations. Perhaps she loved me more for having changed her, but perhaps she simply loved the fact that she was changed.

The varied, but simultaneous, perceptions that Callie and I had—our discrete sense of the world necessitated by dramatic discrepancies in our realities (the sizes of our bodies, the amounts and types of work we had to do, the gaps between emotion and logic, the wiring and rewiring of our brains)—meant that all our interactions, though earnest, were changed a little through transmission. The things we were expressing were always incompletely, even inaccurately, received.

Our brains were changing, independently and in concert with each other. What we perceived and how we understood what we perceived was changing as well. The size of a mother's brain changes during pregnancy and the early stages of motherhood. "We don't know whether it's the experience that changes the brain, or the brain that changes experience," concedes developmental psychologist Pilyoung Kim. Because of advances in neuropsychology, what we understand about early childhood and motherhood is changing.

Because of my changing brain, I understand things differently as well. I am, for one thing, more prepared to interpret—and not to disdain—other people's potentially flawed communications of their capacities, their fears, and their desires. I am, I believe now, more prepared to be accepting of the humanity in all of us. The biggest difference between the smiting God of the Old Testament and the forgiving God of the New, I'd argue, is that the New Testament God went and had a baby.

When Callie stared into my eyes for those enormous lengths of time, it was because she could not take her eyes off me, though the reasons she could not take her eyes off me had nothing to do with what my old self would have understood as an explosion of love. What was happening was something scientists have dubbed "sticky fixation." Her vision (at birth, radically different from that of an adult) was controlled mainly by subcortical brain systems like the thalamus and brain stem. These structures drive the infant to focus on the edge of a field of vision where she can better discern what it is she sees. As soon as four weeks after birth, this starts to change. Her visual cortex begins to dominate. By the age of two months, she might develop neural connections in the visual cortex at a rate of up to 1.8 million per second. (They call such rapid neural development *synaptic exuberance*!) For those few weeks, when her brain changes its centers of vision from the subcortical systems to the visual cortex, there is a contest for control going on between these two parts of her brain. That's why the baby's eyes locked. Not because she wanted to look at me, but because she could not yet control the mechanisms by which to look away.

Childhood-development models like the one I referred to when I wrote of Piaget focused on stages of development. In this light, we move from one stage to the next to the next, changing who we are and how we think along the way. This feels like what it means to be a parent. I am so transfixed while watching one thing that I cannot look away, but I must look away. And the moment I look away, everything changes.

It is true, I cannot fully recall who I was before Callie. I *was* someone before Callie was born, just as Callie's subcortically dominated vision *was* vision. But now we are both fundamentally changed. She couldn't describe what that visual experience was like, just as she won't be able to describe her life without language. She would have to use language to try to describe her life before language, and already, because her mode of understanding the world is filtered so much more frequently through language, that pursuit is destined to fail.

Challenging this system of discretely chronological development—a system well suited to a linearly organized narrative of our lives—the twentieth century child-development psychologist Daniel Stern believed that children *do not* develop by changing from one stage to the next, but in overlapping "domains of relatedness." Once one domain is established, it remains essentially unchanged. Callie still has a thalamus; that hasn't changed. It still relays, and probably partially processes, sensory signals received by the retina before passing them on to the occipital lobe—what we now call the "vision center" of the brain. Stern said, "Once all domains are available, there is no assurance that any one domain will necessarily claim preponderance during any particular age period. None has a privileged status all of the time." Perhaps, as this theory suggests, there is a way of understanding change that does not eradicate the previous reality.

This possibility comforts me. The book you are currently reading dwells simultaneously, and nonchronologically, in different stages of my own development, and of Callie's. When I seem to be focused on a narrative about my daughter's childhood, I might shift to a memory of an event that happened years before I was born because we live through multiple domains of relation at once. According to my father, the retired pediatrician, "Life is not a fixed experience in which only one variable is at play. We might respond to any number of variables at any given time," so that a lack of linearity in the articulaton of experience is to be expected. Sometimes one domain is more dominant than others, but once a domain of relation is available, there is no gaurantee it will ever fully cease to influence us.

Child-development experts like Elizabeth Spelke also disagree with Piaget about the moment of the development of ego and empathetic understanding. They believe that from as early as two months, babies develop a sense of self and the correlating sense of others. Ideas of morality and selfhood that are established in infancy, they posit, do not fundamentally change. When I speak to Callie in a stage whisper on the airplane, it is not just mimicry but also empathy that drives her to respond in a stage whisper. Encouragement of that empathetic impulse might be a key to her survival. As the VA chief of staff suggested, babies must appeal to their communities in order not to be cast out.

I think what we are watching when we are watching Callie is a most remarkable and transparent overlaying of domains. Time is nonlinear within the orbit of the child. At once, and not necessarily in chronological order, she is a mewling newborn, an eye-locker, a crawler, a cruiser, a babbler, a talker, a proto-adolescent, a power player, a mortal body—and all this time, she holds inside her the eggs that could make her a mother one day, as she has made me a mother.

She cannot change, though she is change.

●

AFTER WE PUT CALLIE TO BED last night, we could hear her working through "Twinkle, Twinkle, Little Star." She's getting better with the words. I can now distinctly hear "how I" and "watchu" in addition to "high" and "are."

I notice all these little things she does, each incremental improvement and devolution in language. There were a few weeks back in her twenty-first month when Ray and I tried to record every word she acquired. I was away on trips that were too densely planned and complicated for me to bring Callie, who wasn't nursing anymore and no longer needed me in that fundamental way. Ray stayed home with her and kept me connected by sending text messages that reported her progress. "Add turtle," and I would type *turtle* into the list of Callie's new words. "Add light," "Add wall," "Sticky." I missed her while I was gone, though it was nice to be able to open a cabinet without first having to defeat a child lock.

Now that she's rapidly acquiring language, we don't record each new word as if we are paupers storing up treasure. We couldn't keep up. Occasionally people will tell us the rate at which she is expected to acquire new words. The fact of Callie's acquiring ten to twenty new words each week was once the marvel, but now it is the quality of the acquisition that has me most intrigued. *What* words is she learning, and why?

When I was in high school, we moved from California to Iowa. I lost language for several months, and thus I lost vision. I'd always written. Poetry was the means by which I made sense of the world. But in Iowa, in that new landscape, I had no command of the word. Everything I wrote from August to April was dreck. I couldn't describe anything in a convincing way because I could not understand, could not organize my thoughts around, my new world. In California, grass flourishes in the winter. In Iowa, it fades into a dull dormancy.

Coupled with that dislocation, I now understand, my brain was as different to me as my new landscape. I was going on sixteen, pubescent to the highest degree. As a baby—like all healthy girl children ages one through twenty-four months, my own daughter now included—I had experienced the intense estrogen flood that accompanied the initial expansion of my verbal and emotional circuits. In Iowa, the increased floods of estrogen, progesterone, and testosterone that accompanied my sexual maturation were once again reorganizing the language centers of my brain, just at a time when I had lost my facility to familiarly describe my world. I grew angry and frequently combative, but also, I grew more imaginative, wanting to envision the world not as it was, but as I wished it could be. If I thought I was a poet before moving to Iowa, the move into that unfamiliar landscape at that explosive moment of my cognitive development conspired to assure this was true.

To cleave means both to separate and to draw together. Language helps me to cleave.

3

Last night we took Callie to a little dinner party at a home in the Mission District. Neil, a poet from the North of England, was visiting his daughter and son-in-law in the city, and he invited us.

Neil has met Callie three times now, making an effort always to visit with me on the most convenient of terms. The first time he met the baby, she was not two months old. He took the BART and the bus from San Francisco to share lunch in our Oakland apartment. I was still so frazzled and tired from the birth and the initial trauma of motherhood that I didn't remember that the little quiches I'd bought from Farmer Joe's deli needed to be heated. We ate store-bought salad and cold quiches. Later, when I realized my error, Neil said, "We made do."

I am a person bound to fumble in social situations, and Callie provides a plausible shield. Last night we were over an hour late to dinner. The baby had been napping, and when she woke, feeding and dressing her turned into a bit of an ordeal. I was focused on all of that and never had a chance to call Neil until it was nearly forty-five minutes later than when I'd said we would be at his daughter's house. By then Neil had already called to ask after me, but I hadn't heard the phone.

I said it was because of Callie. I said that I'd turned off my ringer so as not to disturb her nap. I said that since the baby was born, I don't make appointments on time, and I forget to call people and tell them I'll be late. Rudeness and discourtesy—I placed it all at Callie's feet.

No wonder relationships between parents and their children can have so many tensions. I see all of my worst traits coming out more extremely when I am in my daughter's orbit—disorganization, self-centeredness, flakiness, a tendency toward lateness, messiness, a sense of superiority. So as not to be overwhelmed by all the ways our lives could unfold, I often stay insularly focused on my little family at the expense of other's experiences of the world. Romantic comedies tout a concept that falling in love makes you want to be a better person. Having a child seems to give me permission to just be myself, only worse. I am bound to behave questionably, now that I'm a mother.

In the home where we dined last night, there lives a pink cockatoo named Pooh. Ray suggested to Neil's son-in-law, Kai, that this name would confuse Callie because she was potty-training and everything nowadays is about *poo*. Kai looked at Ray with disdain. Pooh was his bird's name. What difference did it make to him that our daughter was learning how to use a toilet? The world does not revolve around our daughter. Large portions of the world couldn't give a damn about her, said Kai's look.

Pooh is a beautiful bird, but loud when he gets to talking. Callie was by turns enthralled and terrified by Pooh. Pooh spoke recognizable English, and that, in and of itself, was probably quite startling. Add to that the volume at which Pooh spoke, the way Pooh fanned his crest, and the occasional shriek emitted by Pooh. Callie kept her eyes on Pooh the whole time she was in his presence, but she never got close.

At one point Kai placed Pooh on Ray's arm, and there he perched for quite some time. I have a picture of Pooh and Ray looking quizzically at each other, both of their heads cocked to the side as if to say, *Why are you touching me?*

After dinner, as Callie started to fade, I changed her into her pajamas so that if she fell asleep in the car on the way home she would already be dressed for bed. The change complete, I brought the baby back to the kitchen. At the head of his table, Kai was engaged in conversation about his years living in Istanbul and his role in the start of the Internet. Suddenly Callie landed on his lap, placed there by Ray. Kai was clearly taken aback. Callie sat there awhile, singing some version of "Twinkle, Twinkle, Little Star" in a stage whisper, until Neil told Kai, also in a stage whisper, that he ought to put his hand on the baby's back, "just in case she decides to topple over."

I've begun to notice patterns in the ways that people interact with our daughter. When she first came into our lives, we had a steady stream of visitors and invitations to visit other people's homes. It was a little like when a friend has returned from an extended trip abroad. People come together to see pictures and pass around artifacts. In this case, the artifact was a very small person.

The more experienced baby people, like Neil, hold Callie and carry on with their business, talking, drinking, and snacking. The baby might spit up on or around them—they remain unfazed. People who are new to the world of babies, like Kai, seem unable to comprehend how to even hold the child. They square off their shoulders. Employ perfect posture. They hold the baby slightly out from their bodies. They fret over dropping the child, hurting the child, and not supporting the child sufficiently, or they assume an infant has the same physical control as an adult human and provide no support at all.

Once, we didn't really know how to hold a baby, either. Just that quickly, we have changed from the sort of people who didn't know what to do with a baby in our arms to the sort of people who tell other people what to do with our baby in theirs.

People ask me how I'm doing these days, and I tell them I've never been better. This is true, though it is also not true. There have been times in my life when I have had a greater sense of order, more control over my finances, a better attitude about my body, a more realistic view of my position in the world, and more time to dedicate to self-care. During those periods, too, I imagine I thought I'd mastered my domain.

·

THE FIRST THING I HEARD from Callie's room this morning were the opening eight bars of "Twinkle, Twinkle, Little Star." The words and the music are coming together. She can sing to the tune and maintain the rhythm, and words like "bymond" and "how I under" are clearly recognizable. Now, when she hasn't mastered a word or its approximation, she fills the space with an imaginative substitute. Perhaps all that listening to the jazz station has been doing something besides keeping her quiet in the backseat. She sounds like I sound in church when I think I know "Amazing Grace" and so don't open the hymnal, only to discover there's a fourth verse that most people skip but this congregation relishes. She chooses a word here and there, and then scats the rest.

Ray had already left the apartment when Callie woke, so I got her from her room and we tried the potty. She loves the concept of the potty, likes to sit on the small training potty we keep on the floor next to the toilet in the guest bathroom, but most mornings she isn't quite patient enough to hold her pee sufficiently long to let it out in the pot. This, too, shall come. I know. And then she will never again be a girl who isn't potty-trained.

So often I think about these things—the things my daughter once couldn't do and then worked so hard to do and then never thought about doing again.

I used to be a woman who was wrecked by nostalgia. When I visited California from Iowa or the various East Coast cities where I lived for a decade, the last days of my trips would be overshadowed by nostalgia. Daily, while I walked the streets of San Francisco, I'd grow more and more depressed by the idea of leaving a state I loved. But I can't do that with a child. With Callie, I am leaving a state I love every day. The grandmother of some kids on the block saw Callie today and said, "When I saw her at Christmastime, she was a little baby in your arms. Now look at her. She's a girl now. You don't have a baby anymore." She is right. It would break my heart if I let it.

Recently, though, Callie has been regressing to her infancy.

She can't seem to eat her morning cereal without assistance. I have to spoon it into her mouth and clean her face when she's finished, whereas if I tried to touch her spoon a month ago, she'd scream at me and grab it for herself, regardless of how slowly the self-feeding was bound to go. It is as if she herself is caught in a web of nostalgia.

This morning she nursed for the first time in three months. After sitting on the potty, she had a lengthy naked-baby period, refusing to let me dress her, wanting to cuddle in bed with the skin-on-skin contact we used to love, and need, when she was an actual baby. I obliged, wrapped a blanket around her little naked body, and lay down, still in my nightgown.

She tugged at the bodice of the gown, like she did back in her nursing days. I told her there wasn't any milk there anymore and asked if she wanted some milk from the kitchen. Usually she accepts that surrogate, but not today. Today she kept tugging. Finally, because I thought I would prove my point better through example, I let her suckle. I knew she wouldn't get anything, and soon enough she'd leave my breasts alone.

After a minute, I unlatched her. "See, there's nothing there." Then I looked down. "Holy cow!" I was too stunned to censor the ridiculous pun. "There's still milk there!"

"Yares till milk ere," said my mimic as she nuzzled back in.

How could I deny her after my lesson had so clearly failed? There we both were, settled into the morning bed as in her first year, Callie nursing and me dozing in and out of a reverie that often wandered into shock.

How can my body be so good at doing what it needs to do to have a child and simultaneously be so bad? She rested on the belly fat I can't seem to lose. When I rolled onto my right side, the shoulder that began to dislocate during the pregnancy slipped a bit. Relaxin, the hormone that helped open my pelvis for delivery, blasted my body with laxity. I have to be conscientious about how I move lest I stretch into dislocated pieces.

I dozed again, exhausted by the work it takes to be a mother, and all the while my body was doing the work for me. By golly, this cow still gives milk.

While I was in Craftsbury Common for the Vermont reading, I was taken on a tour of the Sterling College barn. Two sows had begun nursing their piglets just as I arrived. A flurry of nearly fifteen of the little guys snorted and leaped, racing toward the sows and causing a great ruckus. The barn went quiet the moment all the piglets found a teat to nuzzle. Occasionally a youngster would move from one sow to another, finding a new spot in the rack of the multitude. One sow lay on her side, as if sleeping. Her repose reminded me of my own nursing days, how startlingly relaxing the nursing process can be. Perhaps the sleeping is a way to exit the body even further, since nursing sometimes makes you feel as if your body is not, and perhaps never was, your own.

Within about ten minutes, most of the piglets had had their fill. It was like a grade school cafeteria. Food scarfed, one little pig after another ran outside to play. Two lagged behind, looking for more, but the sows were finished as well. The one who had emitted the occasional snort while the piglets were nursing lumbered up—Lord, she was massive—and took her bull-sized body out of the barn. The one who had been sleeping stayed on her side, but rolled over slightly, refusing access to her teats. The piglets stuck around, working an angle on the sow, but their efforts proved futile.

In a different part of the farm, the sheep were calling their lambs. Sheep only have two teats and hopefully don't have more than two lambs in a season. The lambs found their mothers and butted at their swollen teats with their little lamby heads. Again, I remembered what that felt like, the knocking and squeezing, the urgency of my small, feral beast. The sheep, like the sows, seemed to gauge when enough was enough and moved themselves and the milk source out of their nurslings' reach.

Like the last piglet and a few of the lambs, Callie cried when I ended our nursing session this morning. But within two minutes, she was jumping on the bed, working her hands up over her head and singing, "Itsy bitsy pider uh uh pout."

"DOWN," she said, and waved her arms like an umpire at home plate. "OUT."

I couldn't have staged this nostalgic moment better if I'd tried.

Soon after she finished her regression into nursing, she put on her own pants, left the house with me, climbed a ladder at the playground, and then slid down the slide. She was following a girl four months her elder around the play yard, trying to do everything she did. Today was the day she finally taught herself to work up the pesky inclined tube she had never been able to climb all the way through.

We know what we know. We forget what we know. We know what we know again.

•

To CONCEIVE MEANS to hold something within oneself: possibly an idea, possibly a child, possibly the idea of a child. *Before I had fully conceived of her, I had already conceived her. After I conceived her, it took a while for me to conceive how different my life would become.*

Conceive has its Latin roots in words that suggest the idea of taking something in and holding it. Sometimes when we say *conceive* we mean a thing has been expressed in words. Sometimes when we say *conceive* we mean we understand. We apprehend. To *apprehend* can suggest both enlightenment and fear. It is also a word we use to say we've arrested someone. *Once I conceived Callie, I began, quite differently, to apprehend the world.*

Callie will be twenty-three months old on Tuesday. When we returned to the apartment, she wanted to read *Good Night, Gorilla*, but after opening to the first page, instead of letting me read the book, she started speaking in the speedy way one sing-speaks the lyrics of a memorized song: "Winkle inkle ittle star how I wonder what you are up above world high ike a bimond in sky winkle inkle star how I under what you are." And then, as if that were no big deal—as if she hasn't been practicing this song every day for a little over a month and this wasn't the first time she had practically mastered the whole thing, words and rhythm and tune and all—she turned to the next page of *Good Night,*

Gorilla and said, "epinant," because that was the page where the elephant first appears.

Language is a system of communication we attribute solely to non-infant humans, because we can't apprehend any other system of speech. When I say we are coming, finally, to "speak the same language," I am saying I can, at last, conceive my daughter's world.

TALES FROM A BLACK GIRL ON FIRE, OR WHY I HATE TO WALK OUTSIDE AND SEE THINGS BURNING

I drove into the countryside outside of Appomattox, Virginia. I was going to a party at a friend's ancestral farm. Thick-branched woods grew densely on either side of the road, absorbing all peripheral moonlight. Wind shook limbs until they waved. I didn't recognize these gnarled and night-blackened trees. Now and then something startling broke loose and knocked hard on my rear window, my moon roof, my windshield. An acorn. Maybe a pine cone. A twig. Dead ropes of kudzu dangled here and there, and all my people's horror stories worried through my head. Why was I out in the country at night? Didn't I know better?

The path illuminated in front of me seemed to lead directly to a cemetery. I could see crosses staked throughout the lawn, cut flowers, newly upturned dirt. A white angel guarded the entrance. As I approached, the road turned sharply. I passed the churchyard, the church, more woods.

Behind the big house, I saw them. Though they'd seen me first. Seven or eight revelers, beer bottles in their hands and an old-time country tune still on their tongues, were pointing in my direction. Their bright skin glowed pinkly in the light of a ten-foot fire. They'd been expecting me.

In the broader light I could see bats the bonfire had disturbed. These were their hours to consume.

•

WHEN I LIVED IN VIRGINIA, I associated open fire with historically informed terror. Many of my Southern white friends enjoyed hosting bonfires, but I started to decline their gracious invitations. Though their gatherings often began with a pleasant hike and a lovely dinner al fresco, I could never relax on these outings. I knew the woods we walked through would reveal their malice because I was conditioned to fear. Eventually the fire would be lit and my friends' faces transformed.

For the seven years I lived in Lynchburg, I occupied several historical planes at once. I lived in a community that was legally desegregated and essentially welcoming, but I (and it) retained the legacies of times when liberty was not a given. There had been plenty of lynching parties in that part of the country. I couldn't help wondering, while wandering through the Southern woods, if one such event might have happened on the ground where I stood.

I had no interest in reliving history, through memory or experience. Campfires and bonfires represented a conflation between the natural world and the human. The wood in those piles was innocent and yet acted out a role. Because I was afraid of what humans had done to other humans in those woods and on those tree-provided fires, I'd come to fear the forests and the trees.

•

When the opportunity arose, I left that neck of the woods. I found myself spending the summer at an artist's colony in Maine. There, the legacy of racial violence didn't haunt me the same way. I could hike solo again. Leaf disturbance, the sound of deer in the distance, filled me with wonder, not fear. Ravens warned me off their path and I felt no sense of personal foreboding. I could spend hours tracking wildflowers, losing myself in the dense forest, and never be afraid of who or what might find me there. I was, again, at liberty in the wild.

After a long stretch of such freedom, it began to storm. The rains lasted six days and all the residents of the colony were trapped inside. On the seventh day it cleared. After dinner, reluctant to return to the cabins we'd worked in all week, we decided on a party so we could linger outside listening to the birds, the rustling leaves, and the lapping waves.

The bonfire pit, dug expertly by the sculptor, was perfectly safe. Still, I couldn't get comfortable. All the writers brought drafts to use as tinder. I torched the one about the wild iris's melancholy glister under the moon. I didn't want to write about desperation anymore. The fire warmed all of us, even the dogs. The hound who ran the woods circled me twice before laying its head at my heels.

A painter found a stump that looked like the torso of a man. It had a knot where the navel should be, a twig protruding from the juncture where the solid trunk branched in two directions. There was some banter about the facile ease with which certain artists impress human experience upon the natural world. This was a log, we understood. Still: "Man on fire!" Some of them laughed.

I diverted my eyes from the limbs that reached out of the flames. The hand that extended toward me, whiter than ever silhouetted by the fire, passed me some wine. Everything around the fire was still wet from the rains. We leaned against each other watching sparks join the stars, flying heaven knew where.

Calm down. It's safe out here. I had to repeat this to myself many times.

•

I GREW UP in the semi-arid hillsides of Southern California, where the spark from a campfire, a stray cigarette, a car's exhaust pipe, or a magnifying glass trained on one thing too long could kindle a firestorm that will burn a hundred homes, scorch innocent animals, and demolish thousands of acres of habitat. From a young age I heard warnings about open fires. I was told to be cautious around anything that might ignite and people who find pleasure in starting a blaze. Just as I grew up aware of the historical dangers of being black and discovered outside, I knew to fear fire.

Within the context of my received history I read most words and behaviors as potentially devastating. I know the sparks from any fire might provoke a life-engulfing blaze. History is a crucible, but that night in Maine I realized American history alone was not the root of my fear of succumbing to flames. That night in Maine, I realized that as much as I feared the danger posed to my own person when I encountered white people around a fire, I also feared the sparks that erupted from fire and the violence those sparks could visit on a landscape.

The danger fire posed to a human and the danger fire posed to a habitat: I had conflated these. When I encounter fire, these separate fears become one and the same.

•

YOU'VE BEEN TAUGHT not to play with fire. Your whole life, you've known the rules. When you live in this country, you have to know the rules.

Yucca, ice plant, chaparral pea, bigcone Douglas fir: even the plants here make provisions for flame. There are those that hoard water to make of themselves an extinguisher, and there are those gamblers that reproduce best in scorched terrain. Don't tell me you didn't know. It's inhospitable here, dry and dangerous. A desert unless you own the water rights. Sudden Oak Death strikes and dead limbs litter the landscape. It's a tinderbox, this country. Now look what you've done. The whole family's in danger. The whole neighborhood. Acres of wild country. All the beasts and all the birds. You had to look. You wouldn't look away. A child with a magnifying glass you were. That thin-waisted wasp caught beneath your lens's gaze. When those sparks found wind, you could not quench the flame. And now, this terrifying blaze.

You knew. You know. You've been taught not to play with fire.

A GOOD HIKE

———

Outside long enough, I lose the contours of my body and become part of something larger. What I watch for on a good hike are moments of permission, the times my interactions with what is beyond me provide opportunities to know the world in ways different from how I'm used to knowing it. I lose track of my own inhibitions and begin to wonder just what I might be able to do if I allowed myself the full scope of my potential. I become more willing to test my own limits in these circumstances, and I discover the particular freedom that accompanies physical accomplishment coupled with plenty of fresh air in the lungs. A good hike is an exercise in mindfulness, not just racing up and down a hill, but attending to each object passed along the way: the new goose turd on a boulder that suggests a late or aborted migration; the little patches of lichen clumped along the trail looking like discarded blood orange peels slowly drying in late-autumn sun. When I am hiking well,

I marvel at everything I see and all I am able to do. A good hike takes me places I haven't been before.

Not all hikes are good hikes. One can race up and down a hill in a state of mindlessness that attends to very little. During the portion of the November afternoon when I fractured my fibula, I wasn't mindfully watching the path. If I had become, at some point earlier on that hike, part of something larger, I returned to an acute consciousness of my individual limits the moment I slipped on wet leaves and caught the toe of my right sneaker on a camouflaged root. The single expletive I shouted was enough to make everyone around me conscious of the contours of my body. I crumpled to the ground, said, "I just broke my ankle," and gripped both hands around the site of the injury. If you've ever noticed the way a hurt animal curls around itself, pained and snarling, needing assistance but daring anyone to come near, you have a picture of what I looked like in the Adirondacks that November.

•

THE DAY HAD started off on a good foot. The climb up Castle Rock had been simple and gorgeous, a meandering ascent over orange-gold beech leaves, shallow runoff pools, rocks and small boulders. It briefly occurred to me that I should have worn hiking boots, but this was the only hike I was likely to take in the Adirondacks that weekend and it seemed reasonable not to have hauled my bulky boots all the way from California. My running shoes had grip enough, and truly, this was more walk than hike, our pace mitigated by our numbers.

There were twenty-two of us. Our stated goal that weekend was to discuss how to write publishable explorations of the natural world within the ever-more-complicating context of the twenty-first century. One of our number had written a book called *Sick of Nature*, and one had written *The Secret Knowledge of Water*. One would later die in Uganda, presumably of heat exhaustion, while working on a magazine article about walking the length of the Nile. The quietest member of our group was completing a collection of natural history essays called *Things That Are,* and I had just published a poetry anthology called *Black Nature*. Most of the weekend we'd stay in the lodge, talking about writing about nature. This was our chance to walk our talk.

Matthew and Joe, some of the youngest among us, bounded ahead of the pack, Carhartt-clad legs tackling the terrain with ease. When they came to the caves recommended by Suzy, a lodge volunteer and the woman most familiar with the place, they poked around briefly, then, unwilling to be slowed, sought the trail again and seemed to spring upward out of sight.

I'd started out with these two, excited to be outside in new territory. I marked intriguing sights along the way, that goose turd, for instance, and a particularly remarkable stand of naked white beech, but the pace I kept with Matthew and Joe privileged ascent, arrival over journey. I looked, but I certainly didn't linger.

I couldn't keep that pace for long. I was sharing my lungs and body with a nine-week-old fetus, and my will was not the only power my body needed to heed. This was a new state of being for me. Approaching forty, I had never considered having a child before, let alone experienced the physical and often cumbersome realities of what my decision to get pregnant would mean. I'd always set my own schedule. Now waves of nausea tempered my pace. I was trying not to let discomfort slow me, but concern over how my movements jostled my belly took hold and I was reminded, as pregnancy will remind a woman, that my decisions no longer affected me alone.

As I slowed, then stopped briefly, resumed at half pace, then slowed again, most of my fellow hikers passed me. Soon I found myself walking toward the rear of the pack with the other pregnant lady in our group.

Joni seemed perfectly comfortable taking her time. The path was slippery because of leaf fall and runoff, and she didn't want to chance a tumble. Instead, she stopped periodically and turned full circle, taking in the open blue sky and, below us, Blue Mountain Lake, its dark green water punctuated frequently by small islands and the outcroppings of its ragged shoreline.

Perhaps one day I will be confident and content even while moving slowly. But when we got to the caves, all desire to slow down vanished. The damp, mineral, mossy smell of caves reminds me of my childhood, so when Suzy showed us the passage through, I forgot all inhibitions. I climbed and contorted, grappled and gripped, as if I were a girl again, my center of gravity low and each limb pliable.

Suzy climbed ahead through the first narrow passage, offering the women who followed a hand should they need help. I declined the offer, knowing her small frame was no match for my weight, and aware I could only depend on my own strength and dexterity to pull me up, around, and over the rock face. Despite the fact that my nails had grown hand-model long thanks to my pregnancy, I found holds in the rock. Torquing my knees and ankles, pushing and pulling, and with the thoughtless ease of someone who has been doing a hard task her whole life, I climbed past each of four ever more steep and narrow passages.

Moving through and over rock like that, I come to know it, to feel its sharp points and its forgiving ones, to note what pockets might prove a den for resting creatures and which would safely provide temporary sanctuary for me. Lia, one of the women who moved through the caves behind me, said I'd found holds she'd never have seen. I didn't necessarily see them, either. My body simply knew how to find them. I registered the caves not as a writer, intellectually cataloging the details, but as a dancer, responding physically to what presented itself. I felt like an expert, like the master of Castle Rock. I felt outstanding. I'd forgotten the nausea and bloating of early pregnancy and the trepidation that came along with them, the constant concern over whether I was moving too fast or too slowly or too much or too little for the fetus. I forgot the fetus. I had my lungs all to myself. They were full and my heart was strong.

For the remainder of the ascent I felt good. I felt fit and powerful and happy. I felt like I belonged outside.

THE CLIMB DOWN should have been simple. After a short rest at the summit of Castle Rock, where we took pictures of the bright blue lake below us and of our own smiling faces atop the craggy peak, the whole party turned around for the descent. The pre-pregnant me would have been invigorated by the exhilaration of the ascent. I would have felt empowered and ready to take on anything the world threw my way. But I had overextended myself. I was tired before the descent even began, ready to be off the hill and back in the lodge by the fire. I felt pregnant again, weighed down.

I should have taken care with every step, watching for exposed roots, verifying my footing.

I should have exercised Joni's cautious grace. Mindful of my own body and protective of my fetus, I could have paused periodically and examined leaves and lichen.

I should have exerted a little more energy and stuck with the many paddlers who peeled off the trail and kayaked back to the lodge, completing the circuit I'd started that day.

But I did none of this. I was tired and thinking about the car that could cut out the paddling component and drive us more directly back to the lodge. I chatted with my companions about environmental futures, writing conferences, children, students, the recent increase of human/black bear interactions in Colorado. I was walking in a crowd rather than solo or in a group of two or three, as I prefer to hike, and I was behaving as unconsciously as if I were walking through a park in some suburban town. I was just clomping speedily along, poorly calibrated, and inattentive.

And then I broke my ankle.

•

Kᴀᴛᴇ, ᴛʜᴇ ᴡᴏᴍᴀɴ I knew best in this group, knelt beside me to assess the damage. Kate had trained as a wilderness first responder. She knew what to do when a person was hurt. She wanted to pull down my sock, to gauge the degree of the swelling, but she could hardly pry my fingers from my leg. "I need to see it," she said, looking in my eyes with the reassuringly authoritative gaze of a veterinarian.

"No, you don't," I said. Trying not to refuse her help, but refusing it nonetheless. "It's broken. I heard it snap."

"I heard it, too," said Lia.

This comforted me just enough that I loosened my grip and let Kate do her work.

Lia had been walking about five feet away when I fell. If she'd heard that sound, a sound more solid and interior than any twig could make, what I thought I'd heard must be true. The rest of the way off the hill, while the guys insisted it was likely just a very bad sprain, I assured myself I was not some hysterical girl overreacting to a twisted ankle. Kate seemed worried and—I found this sustaining—Lia had heard the bone break.

As a former athlete, I had experience with both joint injuries and broken bones. I'd already undergone two reconstructive surgeries on chronically sprained or dislocated joints.

During the preoperative procedures for shoulder surgery over a decade earlier, the anesthesiologist insisted I take a pregnancy test.

"I'm not pregnant," I assured him.

"Well, I want you to take this test just to be sure."

"I'm sure I'm not pregnant," I insisted.

"Please, just take this test. Anesthesia is really bad for babies."

I took his pee cup, but not before reaffirming my conviction. "Babies are really bad for Camille," I said. I believed, then, that having a baby would slow me down, keep me from doing the things I felt were necessary for my happiness.

I remained uninterested in having a child until I met Ray, and then it was less the idea of having a child that convinced me than it was the idea of entering this new phase with *Ray*, my husband, in particular. I wanted to create not so much a baby as *a family*. The adjustments I would have to make in my life seemed more manageable with a quality partner. Still, I was concerned about the repercussions of these necessary adjustments.

Sitting on that pile of November leaves, I worried about what would happen to me and to the fetus if I needed some complicated surgery as a result of this fall. I worried because I knew that anesthesia is really bad for babies and I'd believed that babies weren't a good idea for a woman like me. I worried that I had been right to worry about how getting pregnant would radically modify all of my decisions.

But these worries were irrelevant. I had to focus on getting off the hill.

WE HAD NEARLY a mile to walk to the car, and I could bear no weight on my right leg. The first scheme we concocted involved my left side supported by a walking stick harvested off the trail, my right arm wrapped around Drew's shoulder. Six-foot-three, with the build of a man in his late thirties who had played football in high school and who kept himself in decent shape, Drew was the kind of guy you might call if you needed help moving furniture. It seemed obvious that he should be the one to help me.

Unfortunately, though he might have been strong, the one-shoulder arrangement proved inefficient for moving me down the hill. Soon Chip, the next largest in our group, came to help Drew. We discarded the walking stick. The two men now supported me as I hopped slowly forward. As we progressed, the four men in the group rotated positions, Matthew and Joe taking over for Drew and Chip, Drew replacing Matthew, Chip replacing Joe in a round robin game of help haul the crippled girl off the mountain.

I tried to help as much as possible, bounding as high and far forward as I could with each push of my left leg. I lifted my weight with my arms and core so the men did not have to do all the work of hauling me upward and forward. I was self-conscious, wishing I could have been lighter, that I could bear at least a little weight on my right foot. I desperately wanted to get off the mountain as soon as possible, to make myself as light and fast as I could.

I am a big-boned girl—"Thick in all the right places," my

husband would say—and I didn't want to be a burden on the men who helped haul me down the hill. More important, I didn't want to appear helpless. I could play the damsel in distress by letting them be gentlemen who lent me their handkerchiefs and opened my car doors, but I weighed as much or more than most of them, and I was used to taking care of myself. The version of gender roles that rests on a woman's daintiness and readiness to be rescued broke down with me. I think of Sojourner Truth's "Ain't I a Woman?" speech, delivered over a hundred and fifty years ago and still reminding us that the image of women as meek and dainty was a picture of white women. Black women, to borrow Zora Neale Hurston's early twentieth century phrase, have long been treated as the mules of the world.

I have a friend, another African American woman, who is over six feet tall in heels and has the well-proportioned body to accommodate that long frame. She's a big girl, but not fat. When the issue of body mass index comes up, she's likely to fly into a rage. The standard BMI does not take into account muscle mass, bone density, or other, often ethnically related, considerations that might elevate a woman's count. There are several problems with this. One is that otherwise fit women who carry a heftier muscle mass on a thicker frame could easily feel pathological even in bodies that, with appropriate adjustments to the scale, would be well within a normal range. Another dangerous side effect is that women who actually are far too heavy ignore BMI charts and other scales since even at weights that are healthy for their bodies these standards label them overweight. My friend was denied life insurance because a doctor, basing his assessment on the body mass index alone, wrote *obese* in her medical records. I've seen her run her finger across a BMI chart, read where she is positioned despite the fact she wears a perfectly reasonable size twelve dress on her five-foot-nine body, and remind anyone who will listen that for the sake of higher profits in her ancestral past, she was bred to be this big.

Most of my life, my way of dealing with the feeling that my body was outsized or out of place has been to make sure I excel at whatever I ask my body to do. If I could hike as fast, climb with as much agility, ski as competently, paddle as aggressively as the folks around me, I assumed no one would think twice about the fact that a relatively big black girl was on the mountain, lake, or trail. Outside, people only care about size if it slows them down. I tried never to be the one to slow anyone down. This pregnancy, this injury, these put my pride at the mercy of much that was beyond me, and I have a deep aversion to being at the mercy of things that are beyond my control.

The men were all at least three inches taller than I am, and Drew nearly nine, so my abdomen and upper body stretched to accommodate their shoulders as I lifted and pulled myself along the trail. I could sense the protestations of my fetus with every hop and, more than once, I had to wonder how long it would be until I could make use of a bathroom. But my left leg would land, and the men would be ready, immediately, to take another stride, so I coiled my energy and worked to spring myself forward again. This jostled the offending ankle, splinted only by Drew's hand-kerchief, which Kate had wrapped around the injury site and the bottom of my running shoe.

As a five-legged cluster, we often came upon boggy points in the path. At first we tried to hop around them, worrying they'd be too slippery, but eventually we trudged straight through, trying to move as directly as possible. Kate or Lia walked ahead, telling us where the trail grew tricky and suggesting how we might proceed. We'd come to wet or rocky patches and I hopped, with the help of my companions, from one rock to another eighteen inches away. The men grew tired, I was beyond exhausted, and we'd hardly moved two-tenths of a mile.

•

EVERYONE WANTED to be off the mountain, and since the two-shoulder carry wasn't progressing us as efficiently as we would like, Drew suggested he carry me on his back. No one had offered me a piggyback ride since my father, when I was about eight years old, told me I was too big for such nonsense. Still, what would seem illogical under normal circumstances now sounded like an option worth exploring. He squatted, and with the help of four hands, I used my tiring left leg to hop onto his back.

Drew carried me this way as far as he could. Because I had difficulty gripping with only one leg, the women followed behind, supporting my butt. "You didn't think you'd get a butt massage as part of this bargain, did you?" asked Kate.

"Well, I was hoping at least one good thing could happen today," I replied.

Often during this ordeal, I engaged in bouts of magical thinking in which I made no observations but those that increased the hilarity of the situation. I suppose this was my way of recalibrating the scale, focusing on what would get me through to the next moment rather than dwelling on how difficult and painful my predicament was.

Adrenaline, and my insistence on noting all possible hilarity, stocked me full of laughter. I became a best-case-scenario spinner. The fracture could have happened farther up the mountain, on the steep and boulder-laden part of the trail. I might have done this on one of my solo hikes. Then how would I have gotten off the hill? Each time Drew stripped off an article of clothing or one of his outdoorsman accessories, I joked that he was just looking for an excuse to run naked through the woods. I teased Kate each time she braved a peek at my ankle despite the knowledge I'd grown feral in my protection of the joint. I joked about my fetus and how, when it was born healthy and whole, I would play with its little arms and legs, and tell the baby I was glad its skeleton was strong, since the calcium for those bones was borrowed from Mama's. I knew my fetus's skeletal development, though coincident with my injury, had nothing to do with my fracture, but it was a pleasant way to involve my unborn child in our adventure.

People often talk about the survival mechanisms of fat kids, the way we frequently perfect the role of being the funniest student in class. We want to make sure people laugh with us rather than at us. The ego's bruised a little less that way. Though I started out the hike at the head of the pack, proving I was able to keep up with the spriest among us, the realities of my new, enlarged body slowed me, and now this fracture had stopped me entirely. I'd transformed from the fit master of Castle Rock into a heavy, useless burden. I felt awful needing the men to carry me. But instinct, brought on by history and adrenaline, told me that if I couldn't make myself useful, at least I could make us all laugh.

There was still a long trail ahead, and laughter was a better alternative than yelling or crying.

●

WE MOVED FORWARD in this manner maybe fifty yards. Seventy? Then it was back to the two-shoulder hobble. Then the piggyback again, before which Drew removed his birding binoculars, his glasses. Each time I climbed on his back, he walked as far as he could, then we returned to the two-shoulder hobble, letting two of the other men spell Drew as he wiped the sweat from his neck and forehead.

I couldn't tell you how long we kept at it. The men's speed picked up, which would have been a good thing, but for the fact that this sent my leg jostling to such a degree I had to beg them to stop.

Then I came up with the perfect solution.

I collapsed to my hands and knees and moved forward of my own volition. No more jostling ankle. Sweet relief.

"You're going to crawl?" asked Matthew.

"This is going to work. You guys have carried me far enough. I can do the rest on my own. Look, I'm moving pretty quickly."

For a short while no one said a thing. I was clearly set on this solution. I'd left no room for argument, and, it was true, I was moving at a clip that exceeded what we'd managed thus far.

The sun was positioned at the angle where it rests just before it races toward the horizon. All of us knew we didn't have much time before dark.

Forward I crawled.

Chip—the man who had proposed this trip in the first place, the man who wanted to see what the new generation of American environmentalist writers valued most and so invited a group of relatively young nature writers to the Adirondacks for a confab about the future of the genre—Chip looked on at my progress with speechless horror.

He told me later he was terrified some other group of hikers would come along and discover all these white people standing around watching a black girl crawl through the woods.

Chip wasn't entirely off base in his assessment of the situation. Part of why we treat people horribly, why we might make the one subjugated other among us crawl while the rest walk through the woods, why we damage people's bodies, or ridicule them, why we work to break people down, is because we want another human being to give body and will over to us so we can do with it what we desire. Pain, embarrassment, hopelessness, fear: a combination of these can erase pride from a human spirit in short order. Once pride is absent, control is that much easier to command.

Those of us who are conscious of human history know the pervasiveness with which one person's will has been pressed on another's. And as environmentalists, we were all well aware of the ease with which people set up distinctions between themselves and anything they choose to categorize as separate from, and therefore subject to, themselves. What Chip feared was that some outsider would look at our party and assume that a play of dominance was under way. He was afraid it would look as if he were the one working to subjugate me.

Chip was silent on the mountain because his concern about the appearance of oppression was so great. Yet he was able to describe his reaction at breakfast, laughing while he did so, because by the next day the concern felt humorous, no longer a real threat.

The whole time we were working to get me off the mountain, I thought I was worried about the pain in my ankle and the burden of my weight. I realize now that my other big worry, what I feared the whole time on the hill, was that I would have to let go of my pride.

These are the ways human history cross-pollinates with all our interactions in the world. Had Joe, with his Carhartts and Jesus haircut, his Montana roots, his wife and infant child back in northern Iowa, been the one to break his ankle, this essay might have gone in a completely different direction. Or Matthew, the urban homesteader who traveled the world visiting lithium mines in Bolivia and garbage dumps in the Philippines, then returned to Brooklyn to write articles for *Harper's*. What direction would this essay have taken had he been the one transported a mile off the hill? What about Amy, so fine-boned Drew could surely have draped her over one shoulder and sprinted with her to the car? What gendered nuances would this essay take on had she been the injured party? And what racial nuances, Amy being a white woman from Texas, Drew a black man from South Carolina? What do I do with the knowledge that the man I was most able to give my body over to happened to be the one other black person in our group? What if the essay were written from Drew's perspective? The largest and strongest and blackest among us, he was the one who put in the hardest physical labor. Try as I might to lose myself to something larger, I'm always reminded of the boundaries of the body: we are bound by gender; we are bound by appearance; we are bound by race. These are ways human history cross-pollinates all my interactions.

As I was crawling along the dirt path, though, I wasn't fretting about the ways history repeats itself. I wasn't worrying about the suffering the world and I might cause my child. For this brief time, I wasn't troubled by nausea or the pain around my belly. I was just crawling.

Matthew stood above me. "You can't crawl," he said.

"Why not? It seems to be working just fine."

"You'll destroy your hands and knees. Get up. We won't let you do that to yourself." As Matthew spoke, the other men, who seemed to have been frozen by my insistence but who heard in Matthew's words a distillation of their thoughts, sprang into action again, gripped my arms, and pulled me into a standing position.

Forced to my feet by the men, but loath to resume the uterus-stretching, ankle-jostling, pride-crushing shoulder haul, I asked for two of the walking sticks people had gathered as we progressed. For the course of perhaps four steps, I tried to crutch myself along.

The sun was beginning its rapid slide toward the horizon, and Chip would have none of my walking on my own. So the uterus-stretching, ankle-jostling, pride-crushing shoulder haul resumed.

If we were to get off the mountain before the darkness caught us entirely, I would have to give myself over to these men.

I said, so quietly I'm not sure anyone heard me over their panting, "Let go and let gods."

I was being facetious.

I was completely earnest.

I stopped working to lighten their load, an effort that may well have been complicating matters. I revealed the full weight of my body and let the men bear it as far and as quickly as they could. I had to let them take me, and to do this I had to let go of any pretense of pride and control.

The group of people on whom I found myself dependent were relative strangers. And yet, as I was at their mercy in the wild, this was the best group I could imagine falling among. Kate, with her first responder training, kept an eye on my leg and my face, warning the men to slow down if I started to look too ashen. Chip kept a clear gauge on the sun, remaining realistic about how much light we had left and making sure our forward pace kept steady. Lia, who'd heard my bone crack and didn't want me to be jostled any more than necessary, watched our path, guiding us so we could concentrate on smooth forward transitions.

When I asked Drew later if his upper body wasn't sore (by the end of the weekend mine burned from the effort to lift myself as I draped my arms around the men's high shoulders), he said he was actually pleased to discover his exercise regimen seemed to be working. He'd developed what he thought of as a practical workout, training his body to be useful in circumstances such as the one we'd encountered.

I found myself thinking about the urban students I taught at San Francisco State University, in whom I tried to instill an appreciation of the wonders of nature. Many of them were incredulous, even scared. They worried about what might happen to them out there. Mountain lions, rapists, and bears, oh my. I worried about taking my story back to them. What kind of advertisement would I make crutching into the classroom after a weekend of hiking? But I realized that the key to the story was the company I'd found myself among. These turned out to be people I could trust with my body, people who would find a way to get me off the mountain and get me the help I needed. Rather than telling a tale of fear and devastation, I could talk to my students about how affirming this experience turned out to be. I was scared, certainly, but through the journey I discovered I hadn't needed to be.

OUR LITTLE GROUP seemed to be moving along fairly well. I'd given over to the process as completely as I could. Lia walked ahead, charting courses, and I would be lifted off one rock, hauled over a standing pool of muddy water, then set down on a rock several feet ahead. We were moving at a fairly rapid clip, though I did have to pause now and again to let my stretched abdomen resume its normal proportions. The men, even the fittest among them, rotated frequently to prevent themselves from growing too winded.

About six-tenths of a mile into the march, the piggyback, two-arm-carry, piggyback, two-arm-carry cycle ceased to work. Nausea hit me so hard I thought I would throw up all over Matthew and Joe's shoulders.

I had to stop. I had to.

We'd landed in a clearing that boasted a windfall log waiting like a park bench alongside the trail. A grove of trees stood before us, some still decked out in their brightest fall foliage, most leafless for winter. I might have pulled out my camera and snapped several pictures of the idyllic grove, but I had no idea where my camera was. Immediately after the fracture someone else had donned my backpack. Lia had been feeding me water from her own stainless steel bottle. I had no idea whose back my bottle was on. A bobcat could have been walking beside us for the past quarter mile and I likely wouldn't have noticed.

When we stopped to rest, and my nausea receded, I did have a moment to appreciate the beauty of the place. The light was autumnal, slanted in on the grove at such an inviting angle it was easy to understand the trees shifting leaves through the low-frequency stages of the prism, hoping the next shade of gold, orange, or red would effectively catch a nourishing ray. Then giving up altogether, leaves dying and shedding, trees waiting out the low-lit winter bare-branched.

The women sat by me, stroking my limbs and speaking words of comfort. They petted each arm and leg and my head until I began to feel, again, as if these might be my own—parts of my body I could recognize.

Meanwhile, the men fanned through the grove. Men on a mission, following a cue I don't recall hearing.

We watched the men scavenge for suitable branches—fallen limbs longer than their own bodies and thick as a strong man's arm. They whacked these branches against trees, trying to foreshorten them to appropriate lengths. They tore at them to remove jutting twigs. The women, petting and soothing me, laughed about this gendered division of labor as they all but poured unction on the pregnant woman while the four even-tempered men passed into some primal state, sweat beaded on their foreheads and eyes set on securing the best possible stick. They were on the hunt. They hauled logs out of the grove, piling them together for comparison's sake, then held the straightest and sturdiest-seeming branches among them like rotisserie spits while Drew sat in the middle of each and bounced, trying to assess which was the strongest.

The men finally chose a seven-foot cedar pole, about four inches in diameter. Someone's down jacket was wrapped around the center of the branch, and all four men took a position hold-ing it—two on each side. I was brought around to the front. Arms wrapped around the men once again, I was pulled up to my seat on the jacket-padded litter.

Because the path had cleared and widened, the men could carry me this way for the remaining distance off the trail. The women walked in front and behind, checking the path as we went and making sure I didn't slide off the back of my litter. Only once, on a log bridge, did I have to dismount and return to the shoul-der-carry strategy. The rest of the time, we moved smoothly, my leg not bouncing, all four men distributing the work of bearing me. I have no idea if it was hard on the men or not. I suspect it was, though their pride in having engineered this solution might have lightened their load.

As for me, where I'd felt like a burden in those earlier, menial positions, now I felt I was being borne off the mountain with ease. It's amazing what a change in position can do for one's sense of self. I didn't feel like a vulnerable stranger in the woods any longer. I didn't feel awkward or outsized or particularly bur-densome. I felt that, together, we could accomplish anything. I was reacquainting myself with a sense of comfort and security, and also my pride. I might not be master of Castle Rock but, borne on this litter, I felt like a bit of a queen.

DIFFERENTIATION

S ean wants to eat chicken and waffles above the Arctic Circle, so we set out walking toward Osaka in the dark. This is Barrow. February 10. The sun won't rise until around eleven.

The previous day, we'd taken the morning Alaska Air flight that shuttles from Anchorage to Fairbanks to Prudhoe Bay (northern terminus of the eight-hundred-mile Trans-Alaska Pipeline System) and then in and out of Barrow.

Passengers on our flight knew each other—if not by name, then by type. "Those guys from Prudhoe Bay are coming off three-week shifts," said the Iñupiaq woman sitting next to me. "They'll be drunk and rowdy by the time they get to Anchorage." There were families on the plane, but this didn't matter to those oil guys, she said. "How's your mother?" she asked the young man in the row to our left, starting a conversation that didn't include me. I turned to the window and tried to make sense of the tundra well enough to identify the pipeline.

Sean and I were scheduled to conduct a writing workshop and deliver a reading at Barrow's Tuzzy Consortium Library. When we got off the plane, temperatures outside were well below zero. The two of us were greeted warmly by Rita, the library's administrative assistant. She left the SUV running while we checked into the Airport Inn. When she took us to lunch at Osaka, she plugged in the car's block heater.

Sean and I ordered two plates of yakisoba, plus a spider roll and some ikura to share. I love the way salmon roe explode in my mouth, tasting like the ocean would taste if the ocean were jelly. I try to be mindful about my consumption of seafood, aware that the global appetite for sushi is threatening aquatic life—all of our lives, really. But I won't deny that I love the crunch of soft-shell crab wrapped in sushi rice and chewy seaweed. Rita had told us this was one of the best restaurants in Barrow. Who was I to refuse the town's offerings?

After we'd already ordered, Sean noticed Osaka's American menu. "I've got to try the chicken and waffles," he said. "They'll probably just be some Eggos and a couple of frozen chicken nuggets, but I've got to try them."

I didn't want Rita to think we were gluttons. She'd told us the library was picking up the tab for lunch, but said this only after we'd ordered. Food prices in Barrow are exorbitant. Each of our plates of yakisoba was $24, and we had the sushi, too. "We'll come back for breakfast tomorrow," I'd said, which is why we are out walking two hours before sunrise.

Despite a banner on the front of the building that declares OPEN 8:00 TO MIDNIGHT, Osaka is closed when we arrive, so we triangulate back to Sam & Lee's, the red, two-story restaurant we'd passed on our way.

Sean and I take off our hats and gloves in the entryway and peer through our steamed-up glasses into a bright, crowded dining room. People talk across tables like they've known each other a long time. The hostess stands in the rear of the room with her back to us, talking on the phone. We wonder if we ought to seat ourselves in one of the open booths, but an old man sitting next to the hostess looks at us and points to the ceiling.

There is a stairway to our left, but it is dimly lit, unpromising. We look toward the dining room's open tables. The old man points toward the ceiling more emphatically.

We have our pick of tables upstairs. The lights aren't on, and dawn is just beginning to brighten the windows.

"Are we being segregated?" Sean asks as we seat ourselves in the brightest corner we can find.

This is the fancier eating space, like a room reserved for company. "I think we are being segregated," I say, though we both know we are being set apart because we are outsiders, not (just) because we are black.

For a long time, we are alone. I send Sean downstairs, asking him to tell the hostess we'd be happy to move so she doesn't have to turn on the lights up here. I've always been troubled by the resource consumption segregation demands. In the late nineties, I lived for three years in Greensboro, North Carolina, a town of about 275,000 with more than five colleges. One of the colleges had been founded as the state college for white women, a counterpart to the state university for white men fifty miles up the road. Another was founded as a private college for white women. A third remains a private college for black women, and a fourth was founded as the public college for black students. A fifth college, founded by the Religious Society of Friends, was the first to admit everyone. All that brick and all those radiators. The pipes for plumbing and the water drawn for all those playing fields. The multiple libraries, the redundant classrooms. Imagine the resources that might have been conserved if people weren't so set on separating students based on race and class and gender.

Sean returns quickly, without having delivered his message. The hostess is still on the phone. "She turned around long enough to point to the ceiling."

When she finally comes to our table I say, "We didn't want to waste your electricity by making you turn on the lights just for us."

She sets down our water and menus with a grunt, then flicks the lights on as she heads down the stairs. When she comes back, we order eggs, and toast, and reindeer sausage.

In North America, we use the terms *reindeer* and *caribou* interchangeably, or if we do differentiate it is because we call the domesticated creatures reindeer and the wild ones caribou. It is the reins that convert a caribou to a reindeer here in North America, but in Old Norse, from which the term *reindeer* is derived, *hreinn* means horned animal. Unlike other deer species, both female and male caribou sport antlers. Males lose theirs in late fall and slowly regrow them. Rudolph and Dasher and the others pulling Santa's sleigh were probably female reindeer—male reindeer would be without antlers at Christmas.

I've read about people refusing to eat reindeer sausage while visiting Alaska because of their associations with Rudolph and the rest of Santa's crew. But harnessing caribou is not part of indigenous North American culture—rather, harvesting them is. Here in Alaska, great herds of wild caribou move over the tundra, rein-free. They are not considered "labor power," according to reindeer scholar Shiro Sasaki, but are "food material." Caribou are hunted for their meat (which is lean and nutritious), hides (which are used in protective clothing), and sinew (which is used in bows and spears and skin boats). Somewhere in Alaska, reindeer must be farmed for sausage, because reindeer sausage is on every menu. But commercial reindeer sausage is mixed with pork or beef or both, to cut down the toughness and gamy tang of caribou flesh. Sean and I like the idea of eating a local staple, but the animal on our plate, alongside the eggs that had to have been flown into Barrow from Anchorage or the Lower 48, has been converted from a wild creature into something tame as a feedlot cow.

As Sean and I zip up our parkas and prepare to walk into more cold, I overhear a local girl, who appears to be part black, beg her mother to sit at the big tables upstairs. "No," says her mother, pushing past us into the crowded lower dining room. "Everyone's down here."

•

THE SUN IS NEARLY OVER THE HORIZON, and the ice in the distance glows. We explore the shoreline. Where we would find sand in the Lower 48, there is snow and ice. Where we would find water, snow and ice.

Though it looks substantial to us, we know the ice is shrinking and thinning exponentially each year. Polar bears come into town more frequently, looking for places to rest because they've had to swim so far without the ice pack they rely on. Police chase the bears beyond the city limits, trying to prevent the stressed animals from threatening human residents. Sometimes, persistent animals are shot.

The ice has taken on the pinkish yellow cast of the rising sun. I am squinting. "Do you think you would be able to spot a polar bear if one was nearby?"

"No," says Sean. "I don't think I could."

Sean is soft-spoken, and I almost lose his words to the roar of a snow machine pulling up behind us. The driver pauses between two ornamental palm trees, fronds fabricated out of bowhead whale baleen. The wooden house they are planted in front of is gray-blue with well-insulated windows. A dream catcher is hung near the doorway, and next to that is a ceramic cutout of a white whale. I am not sure whether or not I am supposed to experience all of this as authentically Alaskan, but I take a picture to share with my family back home.

"There's a polar bear out there," says the snow machine's driver. He is standing on the footrests as if about to bring his hand to his forehead and scan the horizon for evidence of life. He says the bear hauled up near the college, which we understand is fairly far from where we are now. I ask how he identifies bears against all that snow and white ice. He says their fur is sort of yellow, then he smiles as he revs the throttle and takes off. Looking for bears.

Sean and I want to go with him. We'd love to see a wild polar bear. But neither of us is bold enough to ask for a ride. Instead, we head into the Fur Shop so I can buy a postcard for my daughter.

I choose a postcard with an artic fox leaping in the air over its prey. "I'll leap this high when I see you again, and I might just eat you up," I write on the back of the card.

Sean and I buy hats that read BARROW, AK, to give to our parents. I buy my daughter a compact mirror with the Alaskan flag because the dipper part of the Great Bear is the one constellation I can always recognize, and I think the blue field and yellow stars on the state's flag are pretty.

The flag was designed in 1927 by a thirteen-year-old orphan named Benny Benson, but it makes me think of Karen Nyberg's family. Nyberg is an astronaut who spent six months on the International Space Station last year, when her son and my daughter were both around three years old. Nyberg's husband is an astronaut, too, and on clear nights he'd take their kid outside to wave at the light coming from the space station. Imagine being able to look at the stars and locate your mother. Benson, whose mother died of pneumonia when he was three and whose family home burned down soon after, said the blue field on the flag "is for the Alaska sky and the forget-me-not." We have a world map at our house. Before my trips, my husband and I mark the places I'm going with pins. It's not the same as walking outside and pointing to a beacon in the sky, but it's the best we can do.

The day the director of the 49 Writers reading series contacted me about extending a scheduled trip to the University of Alaska Fairbanks, so that I could read in Anchorage and Barrow, I asked my husband if it would be okay. The hardest thing about accepting the offer was the idea of leaving my four-year-old daughter for nine days. Ray said it wasn't his decision to make, but he thought I would be crazy not to go. I asked him the next day, and he said the same thing. When I asked him the third time—sometimes it's hard for me to recognize his support—he grew exasperated and reminded me that for three of our first six months together I was on the road promoting or researching the books I worked so hard to write. He had no illusions that my travels were going to stop just because I'd married him and had a child. He said I should go, and he assured me he would take good care of our daughter. She was his daughter, too.

In an interview with *Parenting* magazine, in which she talked about leaving her son with his father for the six months she would be on the space station, Karen Nyberg said that "after going through it in my head for a long time," she realized that "this is a dream I had since I was a young child myself. I don't think I would be setting a very good example for my son if I were to give up on my dream." Even a NASA-trained astronaut had reservations about prioritizing her career. For some reason, this is heartening for me to know.

"Those Good & Plenty were three dollars," Sean says as we leave the Fur Shop. "They better be good. There better be plenty."

"Did you buy them?" When he was at the counter, I'd been occupied fitting my souvenirs into my purse, putting on my hat.

"No," he says. "I took a picture."

We've heard that transit costs to Barrow and frequent spoilage due to freezing drive up prices on staple items—a carton of milk can cost thirteen dollars. We want to see this for ourselves. Our next stop is the AC Value Center, the grocery and supply store. I suggest that if we walk toward the church we'll eventually arrive at the store.

I remember the church from our tours the day before. The Presbyterians were the first missionaries in Barrow, arriving in 1890, and their church stands in what I understand to be the center of town. The town's distance signposts are yards from the chapel. (LOS ANGELES: 2,845; FAIRBANKS: 555; PARIS: 4,086; NORTH POLE: 1,250; SOUTH POLE: 11,388).

"If my parents were here, they would have gone to services," I tell Sean. But I'd been afraid the people wouldn't be friendly. "Sometimes these small communities don't want outsiders," I say.

Several parishioners exit the church as if summoned to greet us. One woman stands, arms outstretched and head tilted toward the sky. The white wooden Utqiaġvik Presbyterian Church behind her, she cries, "The sun! The sun!"

In the northernmost town in North America, the sun set on November 19 at 1:36 p.m., and it didn't rise again until January 22, when it stayed up for twenty minutes and four seconds. Each day since the twenty-second, the sun has stayed up longer. Barring overcast weather, which is common up here, we will get six hours and six minutes of sunlight today, nineteen days after the year's first sunrise. "Look at that glorious sun!" the woman exclaims. Then she puts a foot on the running board of a black extended-cab truck and pulls her short body inside.

Sean says, "I don't think we're going the right way."

"The store is just over yonder," I insist, though we both realize I don't know what I'm talking about. We don't even know how to find the Airport Inn.

The sun singer is driving toward us. We flag her down and ask the way.

.

"WHO INVITED YOU?" the woman asks. We are in the cab of her truck now.

Her name is Ida, and though she can remember Sean's name, she calls me Amelia. I correct her twice, and then answer to what she calls me.

"Is there a word in Iñupiaq for when you are speaking to an elder?" I ask. "Where we come from, Sean and I might use *aunt* or *uncle*." Sean and I aren't from the same place, but we are from the same type of people. It would be strange—rude, even—for us to call a churchgoing woman of roughly our mothers' age by her first name, using no mediating honorific.

Our driver tells us the word we should use, but she says it so fast I can't get the hang of it.

"Are you nurses from the hospital?"

"No, Ms. Ida. We're writers," I say from my seat in the back of the cab. "We spoke at the library yesterday."

"Hmph," she says. "Who invited you to Barrow and left you standing on a corner?"

"We wanted to go for a walk this morning," I explain.

"We're doing a bit of exploring," says Sean.

"Whoever invited you didn't give you a tour?"

"We were driven around yesterday," I assure her. "That's how we knew about your church."

She is not satisfied. "You're not going to tell me who it was who invited you, are you? I can't believe they just left you on your own."

"We really didn't mind wandering by ourselves, ma'am. We know there was a death in the community recently and many of the people who would have hosted us this weekend are home with family."

Ms. Ida nods solemnly. She tells us the boy was related. Perhaps he was her husband's cousin's nephew's stepson—I don't remember the whole chain. "I've been at the family's house all week, but this morning I had to get away, to go to church," she says. "When I went into church it was dark outside. Now, look at all this beautiful sun."

For a while after she speaks, we are all quiet, admiring the open sky.

"That's our hotel," says Sean, pointing to the Airport Inn.

"Hmph. They have you staying there?" says Ms. Ida. She keeps driving, pointing out buildings. "This is our new hospital. It's a really nice hospital. When I first saw you I thought you were new nurses from the hospital."

"No, ma'am," says Sean. "We're writers."

Ms. Ida keeps driving in what I understand to be the opposite direction of the grocery store. "My people learn from seeing things," she tells us. "That's why I used to have so much trouble in school. They had us reading all these books, but I never got good at reading. If I couldn't see it, I didn't understand. It wasn't until I started reading the Bible that I learned to really see what I was reading about. Isn't that interesting?"

"Do you think it's because the parables and stories help paint a picture for you?" I ask.

"When I started reading the Bible, the things I read just made perfect sense," she says, continuing to drive. She hasn't answered my question, but she has answered my question.

"Out there is our satellite farm." Ms. Ida indicates the row of satellite dishes at the southeast edge of town.

I recognize the satellite farm. Erin, our host librarian, brought us here late last night, after our reading, so I could see the aurora borealis without the interference of streetlights. Erin had been underwhelmed by the night's show. She'd seen much grander displays. She kept the car running and stayed in the driver's seat. But I was awed by the green light waving through the night sky.

I'd heard about the dancing lights, but I understood the aurora borealis to be a cloud, and clouds in my experience move as if they are solid masses. They do not jump and spin and dive as if each particle is in visibly independent motion, like dancers doing isolations. What I saw, when I saw the northern lights, was an observable enactment of the volatility of matter. In my solid world of cars and books and glasses of wine, I know each atomic particle, each cell and each nucleus, is an independent body engaged in independent, often erratic, motion. Still, the riggings appear so inflexible that I can't apprehend motion. The aurora is the result of particles colliding with other particles and, though each explosion happens in something akin to a unified field, I could observe discrete activity.

I tried to take a video of the lights to send to my daughter, but the flowing tangibility of sparks of differentiated matter didn't convey in the replay.

"That's how we communicate with the rest of the world," says Ms. Ida, driving her Toyota Tundra past the sat farm at the same steady speed she's been driving since we climbed into the truck.

•

WHEN WE FIRST arrived at the library, Erin said, "Welcome to Barrow. Have you already been on four tours?" We told her Rita had shown us around. Barrow only has about forty-five hundred people. It didn't seem like there was much we needed to see. "You haven't really been to Barrow until you've been taken on four tours," Erin said. I thought she was joking, but she persisted. "After your workshop, if you want, I'll take you around so you can take photos."

How to describe Erin? Her energy was a bubble machine of exuberance, and she had a sort of ageless Plains state can-do attitude, the kind I'd come to admire in people from the Lower 48 who move to Alaska and stay.

Her tour of the library started in the children's room: a cozy space with small chairs. Though she made sure to have plenty of Samoan romance novels in the adult collection to satisfy the library's substantial client pool of women from the South Pacific, and she'd organized our event to target Barrow's robust poetry-loving population, Erin was devoted to the children's program. This room boasted lots of children's books and also plenty of YA classics to keep the kids engaged well into high school. She nearly leaped for joy—I am not exaggerating—when I pointed to a prominently displayed copy of *Mama, Do You Love Me?* Set in Alaska, the book follows the adventures of a girl who tests the extent of her mother's love. "I'll love you until the umiak flies into the darkness, till the stars turn to fish in the sky," I said to Erin, quoting some of the mother's lines.

"I'm so glad you know that book!" said Erin.

I told her that, reading the book to my daughter, the illustrations had seemed fanciful, but here in Barrow I'd seen women and children dressed in parkas like the girl's and her mother's, I'd seen dolls like the child's, and I'd seen real umiaks, the skin boats used to ply these Arctic waters.

"It's the best book. I just love it!" she said. Then her attention jumped. "We should show you where you'll be giving your workshop," and she bustled us into a quiet conference room with five waist-to-ceiling windows overlooking the frozen Isatkoak Lagoon.

A group of six children on four snow machines collected just before the lagoon, waiting for something. Sean took their picture. A kid of about five, seated behind his brother, noticed us first. A few of the children turned and waved, looking at us like we were exotic lizards in a terrarium. Sean took pictures until the children bored of us, turned their attention back to the snowfield, popped down over the berm, and drove their machines into vastness.

"This week a boy in our community was shot," Erin told us.

"Yes, I read about it in the paper down in Fairbanks," I said. The papers said the accident had involved a hunting rifle.

"The kids have been skipping school and riding around together," she said, though this was a Saturday. "It's like therapy for them." Erin sat still for a long moment, one of the longest I'd see in two days. "He was a really good kid. Everybody loved him. He used to come to the library a lot. Only thirteen. It's really devastated the community, but so many of the teachers here are from outside. They come to teach, and then they leave when the term is over. They just don't seem to care."

What could we say to that?

"Do you need water? The bathroom? Something to write with?" Erin was up and moving again. "I am so excited you're here. Oh, golly, this is going to be great."

On our second tour of Barrow, Erin took us to stand between two jawbones that arched far over our heads, framing the Arctic Ocean from one vantage, the town of Barrow from the other. "This is the iconic Barrow photo spot. You have to have a picture of yourself by the whalebones." She took us to the Presbyterian church and the nearby signpost with arrows pointing toward the rest of the world. And she took us to Ilisaġvik, the northernmost accredited community college in the United States—the only tribally controlled college in Alaska.

Erin was proud of the college and how it served the community. Signs around the halls were written in English and Iñupiaq, supporting the college's mission to "perpetuate and strengthen Iñupiat (Eskimo) culture, language, values and traditions." We learned from the book *An Artic Year: A Journey Through the Seasons* that the word for February is Siqiññaasugruk. This is "the month of longer sunshine" and a time "to celebrate a successful hunting season." Erin gave us a poster that praised community self-sufficiency. She made sure Sean took a picture of a sign that described what to do if confronted by a polar bear.

Erin drove us out to the satellite farm, past the new hospital, past the ruins of the burned-out Top of the World Hotel. There used to be a restaurant in that hotel, called Pepe's North of the Border, where you could get a certificate that said you'd been to Barrow, the northernmost city in North America. (My grandparents visited Barrow once. Somewhere in their unsorted boxes I could probably find their North of the Border certificate.) Since the 2013 Top of the World fire, nothing quite so intentionally constructed for tourists has taken its place. Most of the outsiders in Barrow are there to work in the hospital or the schools, or they're passing through to work on one resource extraction project or another, mostly jobs having to do with carbon-based fuels.

Erin drove us from photo op to photo op, trying to make sure we saw the best parts of her adopted town. Barrow has its share of interesting human-made structures, including the oldest frame building in the Arctic, built toward the end of the nineteenth century and used as a whaling station and trading post. Not far from Osaka, we saw the remains of one-thousand-to fifteen-hundred-year-old Iñupiaq dwelling mounds. Much later I would learn, from Ronald Brower, Sr., of the Alaska Native Language Center, that "the sod homes are the remnants of a larger community of sod homes that eroded to the sea" and that, in addition to sod, they were constructed out of whalebones and mastodon bones. Standing in the presence of such structures was thrilling. But, for the most part, human construction is not what makes Barrow remarkable. Most of what we saw was human-built and imposed—buildings made from shipping containers or frame structures stilted above the permafrost, which, in this part of Alaska, can be as much as a half-mile deep. Or, like the baleen palms or the jawbone arch, dead things imposed on the landscape. Most of what we saw was desolate, lifeless, and frozen. In spite of this, standing by the bone arch with our feet near the icy Arctic Ocean, we marveled aloud at how beautiful everything was.

"I just love you guys," said Erin. "You are so cool."

We were grateful that she liked us but weren't sure what made us stand out from other guests.

"You'd be surprised," she said. "People come here and hate it. They say it all looks bleak. They say everything looks the same."

"Why wouldn't we like it here?" I asked. Sean and I looked out toward the Northwest Passage, which, somewhere beyond where we stood, was growing more navigable each year.

"The last person I brought up here wrote a blog post about the trip. She said Barrow looked like a bombed-out town after Armageddon," said Erin.

Sean and I enumerated the different colors of white we had perceived that afternoon, the varying shades of blue and gray, the saturation of brightness where the ice sheet met the darkening sky at the farthest point of the horizon.

Later, I'd ask Ms. Ida how she could tell when the frozen field changes from sea ice to land ice. "You can just tell," she said, looking out over the crystallized water.

I wanted to see the difference as easily as she could.

Sean walked toward, or maybe onto, the frozen ocean. At the height of the freeze, the sea ice should be thick enough to support a three-ton whale, but all I know is unpredictable pond ice. I stood at the edge, where I believed the land met the water, too skittish to wander out far.

•

"THERE'S THE GROCERY STORE," says Ms. Ida, pointing to the AC. "Did you still want to stop?" It's a rhetorical question. She hardly slows the truck.

I understand, now that we're in the middle of this fourth tour of the town, that we could have walked to the AC the way we'd been headed, but there were no roads leading in that direction. We would have had to walk straight across the frozen lagoon.

Ms. Ida stops the car at the Iñupiat Heritage Center, next door to the library. I finally know where we are. Erin had taken us to the Heritage Center the night before to see Barrow's collection of taxidermied tundra beasts. Inside, we saw a polar bear and a scale model of a bowhead whale. But Ms. Ida takes us to the back, where women sew parkas and fur hats. Outside, near the trash pile, is the beheaded carcass of a seal.

"Are they throwing that away?" I ask.

"It's storage," she tells me. Today's high temperature will be minus six. Why bother with a deep freezer? I keep being surprised by what comes to seem obvious once I realign my perspective.

In Anchorage, the director of 49 Writers lent me a hat she'd gotten in Nome. It would keep me warm as I traveled farther north. Sealskin on the outside plus a beaver-pelt lining meant hardly any cold got in. Ropes of stiff yarn ending in fur pompoms brought the earflaps nearly to my chin. When we finally do get to the AC, an Iñupiaq woman selling colorful handmade parkas (at six hundred dollars, I won't buy one, though I will be sorely tempted) will ask to look at the hat. Upon inspecting its craftsmanship, she will compliment the maker. I won't admit it is just mine on loan. I like the idea of someone thinking such a fine, warm hat belongs to me. Wearing the right hat for Barrow helps me feel less out of place.

Ms. Ida, too, makes me feel like less of an outsider. Our quickly constructed friendship builds for us a bridge. She tells me she met her husband at a bar in San Francisco's Mission District. I gasp and ask which one. Turns out the restaurant where I first met Ray is just four blocks from the bar where Ms. Ida met her husband. She was attending secretarial school across the bridge in Oakland at the time, she tells us. Sean and I have both lived in Oakland, too. We each know the area where Ms. Ida shared an apartment with two other women, though Sean and, later, Ray and I walked those streets years after Ms. Ida and her husband moved back to Barrow.

"I don't live in California anymore," I tell her. "My husband and I were both offered jobs at the same university. My family moved to Colorado this summer," I said.

"Colorado? Near Denver?" she asks. "My husband was sent to the BIA school in Denver when he was a boy." I have to work that out in my head and am ashamed when I realize I was too dense to immediately recognize the abbrevation for the Bureau of Indian Affairs. "He says they treated him well there." She is quiet for a moment, and I imagine she is considering the alternative treatment her husband might have suffered. I've heard reports. "He has good memories of the place," she says.

In one version of a story told in Sean's partner's family, they say her grandfather's mother ran an Indian school in Denver. Perhaps it was the very school where Ms. Ida's husband was sent as a boy. The Earth is small.

We get back in the truck and Ms. Ida drives slowly past particular houses, looking in the yards. The polar bear hunter doesn't have anything. The body at the Heritage Center is the only seal we see. "I'm going to take you to my house," she says.

Sean says nothing, just slightly nods and looks toward Ms. Ida and also out the window. Later, he will tell me he had been afraid to climb into the truck when we'd met Ms. Ida at the church. Where he's from in Georgia, black men would be wise not to jump into strange women's cars.

Outside the truck window, I can see the lagoon stretch on either side of the causeway we are crossing. I am beginning to understand where we are in relationship to where we have been. Soon we'll pass the jawbone arch again.

•

WHEN WE PULL INTO Ms. Ida's driveway, there are three caribou gut piles in the yard where her sons dressed the animals. At the top of the stairs that lead to the house, her husband smiles quietly, holding open the door to welcome us. Inside, Ms. Ida walks directly to her kitchen. Sean and I linger in the living room looking at family pictures. Ms. Ida with her children. Ms. Ida as a child. I carry my phone to the kitchen and show off the photo Ray sent of my girl at the breakfast table that morning, her cereal bowl just inside the frame.

"I'm so happy I married a Native man," Ms. Ida says of her husband. As she speaks, she chops hunks of caribou with an ulu, a wood-handled knife with a curved metal blade. "We never have to argue about what's for dinner. This is what's for dinner." She walks out to the back porch, returning the caribou, which she's wrapped in butcher paper, to a bench and retrieving some similarly wrapped salmon filets. She also brings in a big hunk of meat that turns out to be bowhead whale. The salmon goes into a skillet, and the whale lands on a piece of cardboard at the head of the table. Her husband puts more cardboard at each of our places. This, I learn later, is a typical way to serve muktuk, one of the local foods Ms. Ida will offer us this afternoon. "Give them plates!" Ms. Ida chides and, without a word, he removes the cardboard and replaces it with Corelle dishes.

Her husband leaves the kitchen and comes back with two lapel pins that announce we've been to Barrow. "I was mayor for about thirty years," he tells us. "Now I'm emeritus."

Sean and I can't quite believe our luck. We've stumbled into a first-class adventure, when all we'd planned was to kill some morning hours. We hadn't asked for any of it, but we're enjoying everything.

Soon Ms. Ida has finished cooking the caribou and salmon, and we gather at the table. She uses her ulu to slice small pieces off the frozen hunk of whale. This is muktuk. It looks like the miniature slices of watermelon I find in my daughter's toy kitchen, a wedge of greenish black skin on a triangle of pinkish blubber. The pink is flecked with bits of black that broke off the skin as the ulu sliced through.

Because Ms. Ida's husband was the whaling captain until he grew too old and one of his sons inherited the position, he and Ms. Ida get the best cuts, including flipper, which is thin and not as difficult to chew as other muktuk. We eat it all raw, like whale sashimi. The skin is the texure of tough calamari, and the blubber melts on my tongue as I chew. Ms. Ida gives us more slices of meat—this time with no skin or blubber. She cuts these from a frozen block of whale steak. Small bites, thin and red like carpaccio, rich with the taste of protein and iron.

I understand this is an experience I shouldn't be having. Or, to borrow an overused word, I understand how unsustainable it would be if a bunch of outsiders, like me, had ready access to the meal I am enjoying.

You can't just walk into a restaurant in America and find whale on the menu. People are trying to make sure you can't walk into a restaurant anywhere in the world and find whale on the menu. For good reason. Whales need our protection, not our appetites.

They are threatened. The ways of life of people whose traditions rely on the animals are threatened as well. I accept the food Ms. Ida offers because I am curious, and because I don't want to be rude, but also because it tastes good, and because I appreciate that my window of permission is small.

•

For centuries, the people who live here have used hand-thrown harpoons and block and tackle to harvest a whale that will feed the community for a season. Nothing is wasted. Whale-bone is used to rig the harpoonists' boats, caribou tendons are used to sew watertight sealskin around that rigging. But, sitting at the head of his table, Ms. Ida's husband tells us the whale hunt might not go well this year. The ice is too thin. Even if the hunters catch a whale, the weakened shelf might not support its weight. If they can't pull the whale onto the ice, it will rot before it can be butchered. "A waste," he says.

Ms. Ida brings out a bucket of seal oil. Suspended in the oil, which is the consistency of what you might find in a stove-side jar of bacon grease, are three-inch-long pieces of dried seal meat. I think it is bearded seal. Left to render in the salty oil, these slabs of flesh are tender, with just enough meaty taste to balance the salt. Seal confit. We dump a spoonful of the seal oil on our plates and rub it on the caribou before we eat it.

While Sean uses one of Ms. Ida's homemade rolls to wipe every trace of seal oil from his plate, she asks me how I prepare meat for my family at home.

I don't cook red meat very often. I think meat is too messy, practically as well as ethically, though I don't tell her this. My squeamishness would ring hollow as I gobble rare, community-sustaining meat off her table.

Ms. Ida is eating a fish she calls cisco. "This is my favorite fish."

"Some people call it butterfish, or whitefish," her husband tells us.

I want to cut myself another slice of muktuk, but when I try rocking the ulu over the bowhead, I find I can't use the knife Ms. Ida wields so effortlessly. "You have to be strong," she says, cutting a few slices of muktuk and handing them to me. Then she slices her cisco and gives one piece to me, another to Sean. "You don't have to like it," she says.

Raw and still frozen from its time on her back porch, the buttery white fish melts on our tongues. "That is delicious!" I exclaim.

I'll look up the Arctic cisco while waiting for the flight out of Barrow the next morning. Like other salmonid fish, it is anadromous, returning to fresh water to spawn. But unlike salmon, Arctic cisco can make the journey from salt water to fresh water multiple times. The fish are abundant in the Beaufort Sea near Point Barrow, where they are a key component in the diets of the Iñupiat of Alaska's North Slope, but climate change and oil and gas development are beginning to threaten their numbers.

Seated across from me at her kitchen table, Ms. Ida cuts us each another piece from the fish on her plate, then offers us no more. She eats the rest herself, popping the eyes out with her Ulu and savoring them like I savored my ikura the day before, like Sean will savor the fluffy waffles and perfectly fried chicken quarter he will order at Osaka around nine that evening.

Sean and I can't stay with Ms. Ida forever, though, sitting in her warm kitchen, we wish we could. We are due to go cross-country skiing with one of the librarians and his friend, a woman who moved to Barrow from Colorado. Thinking we were only walking to Osaka for breakfast and then going to the grocery store we believed to be just down the road, we'd left the Airport Inn without their numbers, but Barrow is small and, without much trouble, our ski partners will find us. Sean and I will stand in Ms. Ida's foyer and hug her goodbye. I will promise to stay in touch, inviting them to stay with my family in Colorado should her husband ever revisit his old boarding school. I will thank her, again, for inviting us into her home. She will tell us, one more time, that it was a relief to have a break from the community's grieving. She will tell me to travel home safely. I will tell her how excited I am to see my daughter. We will hug again, and I will thank her husband for my pin, which is embossed with a walrus, a whale, and a compass rose like the pole star in the Alaskan flag, indicating each of the cardinal directions.

At three p.m., Sean and I, full and warm from our meal at Ms. Ida's, will venture onto the tundra on borrowed Nordic skis. The high fat and protein content of the whale and seal and seal-oil-soaked caribou will regulate our blood flow and body temperature. Surviving, even thriving, in cold climates is the reason people eat such food. Our insulin will release at a steady pace, keeping us from growing sluggish in the frosty wind. As the sun dips close to an orange-tinted horizon, before the first stars appear in the long night sky, we will ski past the mile-long snow fence. When I look to my right and beyond me, I will see ice and compacted icy snow and tussocks of Arctic grasses mounded in snow. My unaccustomed eyes will see nothing distinguishable enough to identify as a landmark. If I let it, the vastness would terrify me.

Out there alone, I would be lost.

All the new thinking is about loss.
In this it resembles all the old thinking.
—ROBERT HASS

A BRIEF HISTORY OF NEAR
AND ACTUAL LOSSES

W e are at Cape Coast Castle, and Callie refuses to be held. She won't let me carry her in my arms. She won't let me put her in the cloth carrier on my back. She won't ride on her father's shoulders. She won't sit astride my hip. She wants to be in charge of exactly where her body goes. She wants both feet on the ground.

I don't want her feet on the ground. The floors of the slave dungeons are caked five to seven inches deep with centuries of hard-packed dirt and sweat and human waste. In one chamber, a drainage canal has been dug to reveal the brick half a foot below. This way, visitors to the former slave-trading outpost on the west coast of Ghana can more fully visualize what constitutes the floor under our feet. What kind of mother would freely let her child walk on such filth? I try to hold her off of the floor, but Callie wiggles out of my arms and runs in circles around her father, our guide, and me, giving the soles of her tiny Keens maximum exposure to the nasty ground. Again and again I try to pick up my daughter. Again and again, she makes it clear she will not be carried anywhere against her will.

It is the middle of May 2013. It is three weeks before my daughter's third birthday and 206 years since the British Parliament passed the Abolition of the Slave Trade Act, in March 1807. The dungeons are museum installations now, part of a series of UNESCO World Heritage Sites dotting the Ghanaian coast. Our guide tells us the castle serves, today, to remind people of the horrors of the Atlantic slave trade and to caution us to treat one another better this time around. To never let slavery happen again. I can't find the energy to remind him that people are still at risk, still being shipped away for profit, every minute, every day. My daughter, running circles around me in her babyGap shorts, is driving me to distraction.

The exterior walls of Cape Coast Castle are brightly whitewashed, so when we walk out of the tropical sun into the male slave dungeons—chambers that are essentially windowless and purposefully dank—we are blinded by the darkness of the place. For extra shock value, our guide turns off a chamber's one dim bulb. This is to help us imagine something even more horrible than what we can already see.

"I don't like it here," Callie says. "I want to get out of this place."

Our guide turns the light back on, acknowledges how uncomfortable these dungeons are. My family is alone with him in this room, having chosen to pay more for a private tour. The guide assigned to us has been leading these tours for many years and is personable and quietly authoritative. He understands what we want from this experience. He asks us to imagine being packed in here with two hundred men, shackled and naked. He asks us to imagine the stench, the vomit, the sounds of writhing bodies, chains drawn against chains. I grab hold of my daughter for a moment. Callie wiggles out of my arms and nearly evades me, but I grip her hand and keep her near. "Shh," I say. "This is a sacred space. Be still."

My husband and I flew from California to Ghana so I could speak at a conference for Pan-African women writers, but also so he could visit Africa for the first time. I wanted to make sure Ray's first trip to the motherland was memorable, and so I'd carefully planned our stay. After several days in the capital city, Accra, we'd ventured to Cape Coast to visit the historic sites where Old World Africans were converted into New World slaves. Cape Coast Castle hosted more than a hundred thousand visitors in 2012, more than eighty thousand of whom were from outside of Ghana. New World Africans are drawn to this site of rupture, curious to stand on the soil where sometime someone who was somehow related to us last took a breath of African air.

The walls of the chamber where we are standing are lined with memorial wreaths, candles, and bottles for libations. Callie runs toward these memorials, then circles back toward us. "She's disrupting the tour," I whisper to Ray as I tug on her arm, trying to curtail her frenzied circle. "She's herding us like some sort of border collie."

This is Callie's forty-sixth airplane trip, so though Ghana is the farthest she's ever been from home, she knows the protocols of travel. On the eleven-hour, overnight flight from JFK to Accra, she ate her dinner, watched the first movie, then crawled into her father's lap and slept until we landed. She knows how to behave. She is no stranger to museums, historical sites, shrines, and churches. She has visited dozens in her short life, and never have I known her to act like she's acting today. She knows she needs to stay near so I don't lose track of her in this strange and crowded place. She knows I would prefer to wear her on my back as we move from one unknown destination to another. She knows how to be quiet on a tour, how to wait patiently next to me while I read informational placards. She knows, in short, how to be the kind of child who causes adults to say, "What a great little traveler you are!" These circles she is running, her refusal to let me carry her, are out of character. After three years of moving around the world in basically the way I've asked of her, Callie is asserting her independence. I do not like it one bit.

I grab her again. She squirms and pushes away.

"She's reclaiming the space," my husband says. "Let her be." Then he turns back to our waiting guide. "Go on," he tells the guide, and on the guide does go, describing chambers that led to other chambers that led to other chambers that led to a tunnel that led to the Door of No Return, where boats waited to carry human cargo over the shore-hugging waves and into the holds of transatlantic slave ships.

Cape Coast Castle was occupied over several centuries, first by the Swedes and then by the Danes, the Dutch, and then by the British. Between 1665 and 1807, the building was constructed, reconstructed, repurposed, and reinforced numerous times, used as an outpost for trading first timber and gold and blankets and spices and then, most lucratively and for the longest duration, human beings. The upper levels of the castle once served as the colonial government headquarters for the British on the western coast of what was then called the Gold Coast but would come to be known as Ghana. There was a church, a customs house, an open courtyard for military parades. There were eighteen-foot walls to protect the castle from the onslaught of the rough Atlantic surf, and lookout posts and cannon mounts to protect the fortification from the onslaught of competing military (and financial) forces. Over time, the castle's stewards built quarters for the colonial governor, quarters for colonial soldiers, and holding rooms for African men and women awaiting shipment to the New World. Up to a thousand men could be held in the male dungeons at any given time, divided among five different chambers. In a different part of the castle, there were chambers for the five hundred African women who, our guide points out, added their monthly blood to the filth that soiled their chambers' floors.

Cape Coast Castle prepared fifteen hundred African men and women at a time for transit to colonies in the New World. Men, women, and children from throughout the interior and the coast. Men, women, and children from many tribes and nations, many language groups. Fifteen hundred, and then another fifteen hundred, and then another fifteen hundred, and another, month after month, year after year, decade after decade, for more than 150 years. Most of the West Africans who ended up in the British colonies in the Americas passed through the castle at Cape Coast. Millions of Africans who ended up in the Americas passed through these dungeons. Visiting Cape Coast Castle, for a New World African, is, in a most distressing way, like coming home.

I have been here once before, in 2003. After that visit to Cape Coast and Elmina, the coast's original slave castle farther west, I had lunch with Ama Ata Aidoo, one of Ghana's leading writers. "Tell me," she asked, "what did you think?"

I remember being quiet for longer than seemed polite. I was trying to formulate an answer to her question. "Honestly," I told her finally, "I don't know what to think. It was all so overwhelming."

"Good," she said. "That's good. I've lived in the shadow of those castles my whole life, and I still don't know what to think about them. If you had words already, I'd say you weren't thinking hard enough."

I didn't feel Ray should travel to Ghana without visiting the castles, and I didn't want him to have to go alone. So the whole family went together. I had been curious to see if the castles would be different the second time around, but nothing had changed since I'd visited them a decade ago. I am still awed by the experience of standing on this polluted ground.

This time, though, I have my daughter with me. I am trying to make sure she behaves like a civilized girl, and I am also trying to push back waves of terror that overcome me when I think about what it would have been like to be a mother here, terrified not only for my own life, but also, I understand palpably now, for my child's.

In Elmina, the day before, Callie first demonstrated her refusal to be carried. The Pan-African women's conference had arranged a tour of the Portuguese stronghold as an extension of the week's historic and literary explorations. When the thirty-person group we were part of stopped in the women's holding pen, Callie ran in circles around everyone. Some women appeared not to notice her at all, some actively ignored her, but a few women smiled and held out their hands for Callie to slap as she neared them.

Part of me welcomed my daughter's wild behavior. My reactions to Elmina were muted because I was focused on Callie, trying to rein her in, trying to keep her from infringing on the other travelers' experiences.

The tour of Elmina progressed from one horror to the next. Our group stood in the courtyard in front of the women's holding pen learning about the well that held disease-laced water in which particular women were made to bathe before they were sent up to the governor's quarters where they could be used by any man whose path they crossed. I was busy keeping my daughter from the well's open pit. All my attention was focused on her body. Though I heard what the guide was saying about all the other bodies that had been in jeopardy right where I was standing, I also couldn't really hear him because I was too busy worrying about what might happen to my girl.

She and I split from the group and climbed the stairs to the governor's chambers. Callie has always loved stairs, and letting her climb them was the best diversion I could come up with. Outside of the castle would be worse than inside. Hawkers and grifters patrolled the exterior courtyard waiting to beg money from foreigners whose wealth, even when meager, was exponentially more than theirs would likely ever be. The taxi we'd hired to ferry us between our resort hotel and Elmina was parked some distance away, and walking into those crowds to find it would mean fending off dozens of men, women, and children practiced in the art of extracting money through guilt and manipulation. My husband was still on the tour and would be for some time. Since nothing was air-conditioned in that part of the country, including our taxi, the coolest, most comfortable place to wait for him was inside the castle. Upstairs, in a room with walls yellow as a child's painting of the sun, Callie could move freely. In the governor's quarters, she ran circles around the site that would have held the governor's bed, a bed into which centuries of African women were forced for the pleasure of the men in charge.

"This is really out of character for Callie. She doesn't usually run around like this," I said to a woman who'd broken from the larger group and joined us upstairs. She was a poet from Harlem. Callie and I frequently spend time with her when I travel to New York for speaking engagements. I said, as much to convince myself as to remind my friend LaTasha, "She's usually incredibly well behaved."

Callie ran in circles and circles and circles around the room, and when she finished her circles she ran to the big window that looked out over the exterior courtyard and down to the sea. "There!" she said, pointing to our taxi driver. He was standing just apart from a crowd of local men, watching fishermen paddle their boats toward the shore.

"That's right, mamí," LaTasha told Callie, using the endearment acquired from neighbors who came to New York from stops on the diaspora like Puerto Rico, the Dominican Republic, and Cuba. "It's never too early to plan your escape."

"There," Callie said, pointing toward the ocean and our driver once more.

Later that morning, our guide walked us to Elmina's interior courtyard. He was going on about military exercises and other late colonial uses for the space when Callie broke free from my grip and ran toward a set of stairs on which an elder member from our group sat. She was an African American woman who spent half of each year living in the Republic of Benin, 280 miles northeast on the old Slave Coast. She was wearing a dress and head wrap made from West African wax-print cloth. Callie sat beside the woman with her feet together. She placed her hands, palms up and open, on her lap. "Auntie," my daughter said, though we'd not directly taught her to use that honorific with a stranger, "I'm hungry. Do you have any food?"

Callie had been asking me for food since we arrived at Elmina, but I'd brought no snacks, thinking it would be disrespectful to eat in a place where so many people were tortured, some unto death. I had a lot of ideas about propriety, and Callie was resisting nearly all of them. Auntie dug in her purse and came up with a toffee, which she taught Callie how to suck without swallowing and which stemmed my girl's hunger and her wandering focus until I could get her back to the hotel for a proper meal.

"This one knows how to take care of herself," the woman said to me. "She'll be okay, no matter what happens." Then she pressed her cane against the castle steps, strained into a standing position, and walked away.

I think of these words now, in one of the men's dungeons in Cape Coast Castle, Callie primed to run circles around her parents and our guide. Maybe my husband was right: she is reclaiming the space. Maybe Auntie was right: Callie is taking care of herself. I decide to let her go, to let her direct her own movements. She circles the three of us, and I falter in my certainty. I look at our guide to see if I should do something to stop her.

"She's not bothering me," says the guide.

"Let her be," says my husband.

We are in the last accessible male dungeon. The guide is orienting us, pointing out the passageways between chambers, and then making sure we see the wall on the ocean side of this chamber that interrupts these connections. In front of that wall is an altar on which a priest is quietly seated. After all the wreaths and offerings, I am not particularly surprised to see a priest waiting on an altar. "There used to be a tunnel there," says the guide, pointing to the blocked-off area behind the altar. This history lesson will go on, the guide's uninterrupted speech indicates, regardless of my concerns about my daughter, regardless of the presence of a priest. "That tunnel led to other chambers and eventually to the Door of No Return. The British sealed that tunnel in 1807 to symbolize the end of the slave trade. Never again would a person have to walk through that tunnel to the waiting ships," he says. Callie circles and circles and circles. Then she stops.

She stands in front of me now, watching the priest. The priest is dressed in a traditional manner, a cloth draped over one shoulder. He is holding something in one hand that looks like a feather-tipped wand. His sandals are at the foot of the altar. His feet are bare. He has his back to the sealed tunnel and is facing in the direction of the chambers through which we've come. He does not seem to be looking at anything at all. The wall opposite him, maybe. Maybe something inside the wall, or something beyond it, but nothing I can discern.

Now our guide is nearly finished in this room. "People leave offerings here," he tells us, acknowledging for the first time the wreaths and flowers and bottles we've seen lining the walls. Then he is quiet, as if he expects us to make an offering as well.

"Thank the man for his important work," I tell Callie, because I think the priest's important work is to absolve the horrors of slavery. I should thank him myself but choose, instead, to send Callie. I will wonder, later, if this was a mistake or a godsend. I know there is very little I can do to change the course of history, but later I will reflect on all the decisions I made while I was on that coast. I will wonder if I made a huge mistake going to that coast at all. Right now, though, all I do is ask her to thank the man for his important work.

Rather than muffling her thank-you in her shoulder, as young children often do when asked to acknowledge strange adults, Callie stands up straight, looks directly at the priest, bows, and says, "Thank you." Crisply, cleanly, loudly. I think she repeated this seven times, but when I tell the story to my mother on our cheap international cell phone later that night, Callie will correct me. "No, Mommy, five times." She will say this with authority, though she will not dwell on the issue any longer than required. "I did it five times."

As we leave the dank confines of the chamber and walk out into the Atlantic coastal air, our guide will tell us the priest back in the dungeon serves a local god. The castle and its dungeons were built over the place where the god lives, but the god did not move, even after all the things that happened here. Now that the castle is open to the public, a local priest has set up his altar. He returns, regularly, to honor the god, and people come for blessings and to give offerings.

When Callie says her five thank-yous, I watch the priest, who watches my girl. When she is finished, he gives her a nearly imperceptible nod. I will wonder about this later, but at the moment I am simply amazed.

•

THREE DAYS LATER, we are staying in the African Rainbow Resort at Busua Beach, seventy miles southwest of Cape Coast. The shore is shallow here, the currents calmer.

The night after Cape Coast Castle, Ray and I ask Callie to tell us her favorite thing about the day. We ask this of her nearly every day, so we don't think about how difficult a question it might be after a day spent in a 350-year-old dungeon. Callie doesn't hesitate, though, to describe her favorite thing. "Visiting my imaginary castle that wasn't scary," she says.

"Yes," I say. "I guess the real castle we visited was pretty scary, wasn't it?"

"Mmm-hmm." We are at dinner. She is eating french fries.

After a moment's hesitation, she puts down her fry so she can say the rest of what she needs to say. Her hands fly up as if she is holding scales of justice, one palm up to the right of her head, one palm up to the left. Between each clause she pauses, as if considering her options. She shrugs her shoulders, lifting both hands simultaneously, before continuing. "There are only a few things you can do when you are someplace really scary," she says. "You can play or . . . be confused or . . . do something. . . . Or read a book." Then she drops her hands and focuses on her fries.

This girl is three weeks shy of her third birthday, and already she knows how to address priests of the ancient order. She knows that a sacred number in Ifá, a dominant religious tradition of West Africa, is five, not seven, the sacred number of Christianity I'd attempted to impose upon her. I hadn't explained slavery to her, could not explain slavery to her, but she knew how to deal with the stress of being asked to thank a priest who may or may not have been cleansing a site of centuries of trauma. We put her in positions where she had to take care of herself despite, and sometimes because of, our well-laid plans. I feel awful that I put my baby girl in a situation where she had to define her coping strategies so specifically. Ray and I determine, immediately, that the history portion of our Ghanaian tour is over. We are finished with slave castles and slave forts and slave dungeons and trading ports where the commodities of trade were human beings. We are going to relax on the beach.

At Busua, the beach extends a long way out, maybe a hundred yards, with hardly any increase in depth. This means that even at high tide my husband and I can safely walk out quite a distance. The waves come in sets of two. One wave takes the water level from waist-high to shoulder height, then seven or eight beats of calm, a slight undertow, nothing too dramatic, then another wave takes the water level from waist-high to shoulder height. Perfect bobbing conditions.

At other beaches on the Ghanaian coast, I kept a firm grip on Callie's arm, but here we frolic. I am not scared. Ray's got our daughter on his back. He's holding her with one arm, and she's holding him around the neck. Callie has finally agreed to be carried. She is going where she wants to go and how.

We bob when the swells come; we're a good twenty feet from where the waves are breaking. We are laughing. We are not thinking about any of the horrible things we've been thinking about for the last several days. One wave takes the water from waist-high to shoulder height, then seven or eight beats of calm, a slight undertow, then the water swells from waist-high to shoulder height. We come together again as a family. We are all happy. We are feeling clean, finally, in this warm water. Callie is on her father's back, and I am beside the two people I love most. One swell takes the water level from waist-high to shoulder-height, a slight undertow, then I look up at the twelve-foot wave that is breaking over our heads.

When I come up for air, I look immediately for Ray. He does not have our daughter on his back, or in his arms, or anywhere near.

"Where's the girl?" I shout. I am so frightened I can't remember the name we chose for her.

"I'm looking for her!" my husband shouts back. I am swimming toward where he's standing, and we both see her, then, sinking just under the surface, legs toward the ocean floor, arms floating out to her side, chin tucked into her chest, like she's been crucified in the water.

He grabs her out of the ocean, and we head toward the shore. Callie is coughing now, thank all the gods. No one says anything. We are just listening to the sound of the air coming in and out of her lungs.

We reach the beach and collapse on the wet red sand. Callie looks around and stands up. She walks higher up the beach to where the sand isn't wet anymore, and then she sits, her legs planted firmly on the ground, running her fingers through the dry sand, staring at the ocean she narrowly escaped.

I pride myself on being a California girl, the sort of girl who has mastered knowledge of the ocean. I'm used to gleaning meaning from the patterns of waves. I counted some sets and trusted, from this history, that I could predict the future, forgetting what a longer view of history could teach me.

When we leave Busua and travel back to Accra, we stay a few nights with a woman who taught for years at the university in Cape Coast. We tell her what happened to Callie in the water, and she is horrified. "You have to be very careful swimming in those waters," she tells us. "All the time people are lost to the Atlantic. All the time."

Of course. Of course. We know this. How many centuries of parents have lost their children along that voracious coast? São Jorge da Mina Castle, the first of the castles, was built by the Portuguese in 1482, first for the extraction of gold and then for the extraction of human beings. By late 1637, St. Georges of the Mine Castle, or Elmina, as it came to be known, was under the control of the Dutch West India Company, one of the most rapacious slave-trading outfits in the world. Elmina, Cape Coast Castle, Fort Metal Cross. Fort Amsterdam is in the same village as the resort where we stayed while we visited Cape Coast and Elmina. Fort Christiansborg, now known as Osu Castle, has served as the seat of government in Ghana in recent years. Fort Santo Antonio, Fort Vredenburgh, Fort San Sebastian, Fort Batenstein, Fort Patience, Fort William, Fort Orange, Fort Apollonia, Fort Good Hope. We could have visited more than twenty-eight slave castles and forts along the coast of Ghana, but we'd thought for a few days we could get away from all that fetid history and play, carefree, in the ocean.

At Busua, just out of sight of Fort Metal Cross, we sit with Callie and watch the water for a good five minutes until she finally breaks the silence, says, "That was a really big wave," and we feel, again, the coastal African sun as it beats on us, warming and also darkening our skin.